NATIVE AMERICA

NATIVE AMERICA

Arts, Traditions, and Celebrations

By Christine Mather

Photographs by Jack Parsons

Design by Paul Hardy

Clarkson Potter/Publishers
New York

To Becky Parsons and
Davis Mather, with love

A list of photograph credits appears on page
240.

Published by Clarkson N. Potter, Inc.,
distributed by Crown Publishers, Inc., 201 East
50th Street, New York, NY 10022

CLARKSON N. POTTER, POTTER, and
colophon are trademarks of Clarkson N. Potter,
Inc.

Manufactured in Japan

Library of Congress Cataloging-in-Publication
Data

Mather, Christine.
    Native America: arts, traditions, and
celebrations/by Christine Mather;
photographs by Jack Parsons; design by
Paul Hardy.—1st ed.
        p.   cm.
    1. Indians of North America—Social life
and customs. 2. Indians of North America
—Art.   I. Title.
E98.S7M25 1990
306'.08997—dc20   90-7059
                                            CIP

ISBN 0-517-57436-5

10 9 8 7 6 5 4 3 2 1
First Edition

ACKNOWLEDGMENTS

The people whose help is acknowledged herein represent in many ways a roundup of those dedicated to the preservation, continuation, and well-being of Native American art. There are many hundreds more out there whom time kept from us. Behind each of the photographs printed and the many hundreds more that couldn't be, there is a story of generosity of spirit that made this publication possible.

Of the many important institutions that have worked to preserve and protect Native American art and culture, we should like to thank especially those who shared their valuable resources with us: the Thomas Gilcrease Institute of American History and Art, Tulsa, Oklahoma; the Photo Archives and Fine Arts Museum of the Museum of New Mexico, Santa Fe; the Southwestern Association of Indian Affairs, Santa Fe; the Millicent Rogers Museum, Taos, New Mexico; the Montana State Arts Commission; the Kootnei-Salish College, Montana; the State Arts Council of Oklahoma; Makah Cultural Center, Neah Bay, Washington; Thomas Burke Memorial Museum, Seattle, Washington; Native American Center of the Living Arts, Niagara Falls, New York; Museum of American Folk Art, New York City; Woodland Indian Cultural Educational Center, Brantford, Ontario; Anthropological Collections of the Royal British Columbia Museum, Victoria; U'Mista Cultural Center, Alert Bay, British Columbia; Cherokee Heritage Center, Tahlequah, Oklahoma; Hubbell Trading Post National Historic Site, Ganado,

Arizona; University of British Columbia Museum, Vancouver; American Indian Archaeological Institute, Washington, Connecticut.

Among the listing of many sensitive and adventurous art dealers, art galleries, and art collectors a number of names are absent at their request: Glen Green Gallery, Marilyn Butler Gallery, Robert Nichols and Jonathan Parks, Ray Dewey, Rick Dillingham, Joe Carr, Benson Lanford and Robert Gilmore, Jordan Davis and Morning Star Gallery, Will Channing and Spencer Throckmorton at Channing-Dale-Throckmorton Gallery, Natalie Linn, Tony Isaacs, Indian House Records, Joshua Baer Gallery, Leona Lattimer Gallery, Mark Winter of the Durango Collection, Nedra Matteucci and Forrest Fenn of Fenn Galleries, Lane and Janie Coulter, Chris Selser, the Pendleton Store, Sandra Martinez and Dave Rettig at Martinez and Rettig Gallery, Tobe Turben Trading Post, Richardson's Trading Post, Doug Allard, John Kania Gallery, Dick Howard, Mr. and Mrs. David Silver, Mr. and Mrs. Arturo Ramos, Tukey Cleveland, Joe Atkinson of Cameron Trading Post, Jackson Clark of Toh-Atin, Dennis and Janis Lyon, Jack Silverman, Mr. and Mrs. Bill Holm, Mr. and Mrs. Charles Aberle, Dr. Harry Deupree, Mr. and Mrs. James Havard, Mr. and Mrs. Harvey W. Johnson, and Letta Wofford.

Our encounters with artists and their works enriched this book immeasurably. We thank each of them for their dedication and generosity: Dan Namingha, Elwood Green, Manfred Susunkewa,

Sankey George, Jr., Fermina Banyacya, Isabel John, Mae Jim, Fannie Mann, Geanita and Angelita John, Agnes Kenmille, Patricia McClure, Dwight Billedeaux, Douglas Glenmore, Johnny and Joan Arlee, Mavis Doering, Anna B. Mitchell, Peter B. Jones, Spencer McCarty, Don Lelooska, G. Peter Jemison, David Bradley, Denise Wallace, Rovena Abrams, Calvin Kettle, Doug Hyde, Ann Green, Tony Price, Louise Henry, Tony Hunt, Jackie Stevens, Helen Cordero, Rhonda Holy Bear, Jaune Quick-to-See Smith, Robert Davidson, Eileen and George David, Dorothy Grant, Cippy Crazy Horse, Bill Reid, Greg Colfax, Harold Littlebird, R. C. Gorman, Allan Houser, Emmi White Horse, Bob Haozous, Frank La Pena, Mary Lewis, Ramona Sakiestewa, Gail Bird and Yazzie Johnson, and Tessie Snow.

While on the road, we were helped by many who gave us names, information, and often a place to spend the night. A special thanks to them for looking out for us: Ramona Sakiestewa, Jack Loeffler, Kelcey Beardsley, Vicki Davis, Barry and Nicki Abrams, Frank Clifford and Barbara Anderson, Buzz and Cathy Mather, Betty Price, Nona Jean Hulsey, Linda Braken, Joan Marron, Charmay Allred, Susan McNeill, Steve and Linda Nelson, Corky Claremont, Katherine George, Putt Thompson, Robin Lill, Lucia Balinbin, John Schroeder, Kitty Belle Deernose, and Doug Allard. Joe Adkinson at the Cameron Trading Post and R. A. Naile of the Fred Harvey Company at the Grand Canyon were more than generous with their accommodations.

The comprehensive sources could not have been compiled without the assistance of my old college chum Roberta Cantow and my mother, Genne Regas.

The author and the photographer wish to thank Fuji Photo Film U.S.A., Inc., for their contribution of film used in the production of this book and for their interest and faith in the project.

We began working on this project in 1987. There are those who really stuck with us through those initial formulative days. Our thanks to Nancy Novogrod and Burt Tauber, who supported us at the beginning. Our agent Deborah Geltman is a positive and knowledgeable person who has given us great confidence and sound advice. At Clarkson N. Potter, Carol Southern and Gael Towey contributed greatly to the ongoing process of preparing this publication. We were grateful that Paul Hardy embraced this project; with his great skill as a designer we felt we were in the best of hands. To Lauren Shakely, editor and friend, all the thanks that accrue to one who works always in our best interest, with such good grace and humor, are due. Many others at Potter deserve our thanks.

All our love to our children: Jack's big boys Alex and Chris and my little girls Amanda and Thais. My parents, Chris and Genne Regas, helped in so many ways materially and spiritually that it would not be an overstatement to say that this publication is in many ways due to their support. Our love and thanks to our spouses.

Christine Mather, Jack Parsons, Santa Fe

CONTENTS

INTRODUCTION

O ur search for Native America was a search into the very origins of our country, our national spirit, and our unique heritage—and a look at the inheritors and contributors to this legacy, the original inhabitants of this land. There is no corner of North America that has not been influenced by Native Americans: the island of Manhattan, once crisscrossed by Indian trails, may all but have obliterated its Indian heritage, but farther west a real trail of influence becomes apparent. At the outer reaches of the westward expansion of the pioneers, the settlements of Pueblo Indians in the Southwest set the tone for life in that region. In California the trail becomes obscured by the wild growth of the 20th century; it is hard to see and imagine that centuries ago the area served as home for countless hunting and gathering groups that thrived on the riches of its valley and coastal regions. On the Northwest Coast, the arbitrariness of the political boundaries between Canada and the United States are made obvious by the fishermen, hunters, and wood-carvers whose common ancestors gave to our two countries outstanding art and cultural traditions. Between the two coasts, and beyond the once tree-covered lands of the Middle West, were the grasslands and the mystic warriors whose intensity and integrity forever captured the imagination of the world at large and fueled much of the romance and legend of the American West. Some of these people are gone but they are not forgotten; the land bears their memory.

The interrelationship of man with landscape is so intense and of such long standing in Native America that it is impossible to see parts of the landscape without seeing and reliving the accumulation of human history upon the land. Ritualized behavior, ceremony, mythology, worship, totem, superstition, and legend—all are part of the ongoing quest for meaning that characterizes Native American life. The spires of rock, the whirlwinds, the clouds, water, and mountains became the gods, the homes of the gods, or even the place from which man finally emerged to take his place upon the earth. From these myths of Creation came not only the vital information concerning locale but also the ceremonies of Native American life. Ritualized dance and music followed and conformed to the legends; they provided the means by which the legend and myth could be acted out by the living peoples. Sacred locations, important symbols, costume, and masks contributed to the many layers of myth.

M uch of the legacy of Native Americans is tied to their relationship to the land, but it is also equally tied to the plants and animals that once populated the land in such abundance. The entire framework of life focused upon the reverence for nature's gifts and the learning of the lessons it had to offer. This approach seems fundamental now, and harmonious in comparison to the precepts of Western man. The waters of Chesapeake Bay teemed with aquatic life, millions of buffalo crossed the Great Plains, and masses of passenger pigeons blocked the light from the sun. When we contemplate the hole in the ozone layer, acid rain, polluted waterways, eroded land, and endangered species, we cannot help but yearn for the return of the land that was once the home of Native Americans.

So deep was the Native American's reverence for the earth that an animal life was not taken or a seed

Frontier photographer Ben Wittick preserved the faces of the people of the pueblos: a Hopi girl, Ng-Nue-Si, *above right,* and a couple from Laguna Pueblo, ca. 1882, *above.* The Cherokee Heritage Center has re-created the past in an outdoor "living" museum in Tahlequah, Oklahoma, *below right.* The Grand Canyon in Arizona, *opposite,* offers yet another dimension of time, of man's brief sojourn upon the land.

planted without reference to their place in the cycle of life and death of which man was but one small part. Each individual felt a bond with the elements of nature, and often even had a bond to an animal through the symbolic kinship of clan. The unique spiritual connection between Native Americans and the natural world deeply impressed the first Europeans in the New World, who lamented the intuitive harmony with nature that had been lost to Western man. Native Americans served as pathfinders for the first colonists, introducing the ways of this New World, the plants and animals that inhabited it, and the names of its mountains, rivers, and plains. It is not surprising that our annual national day of giving thanks is a celebration not only of harvest, but of a harvest gathered from the new land with the help of its original dwellers. More interesting, though, is the explicit preference for maintaining the place names of the natives: Michigan, Ohio, Minnesota, and Mississippi—all could have had prosaic names had not American colonists fallen in love with the sounds and idioms of the New World. Where else but in America can you hop into the Pontiac in Penobscot? The lure of the land becomes inextricably tied to the people who knew it best. And the people who inhabited the land were as varied and diverse as the types of terrain and environments of the North American continent.

Yaqui and Maidu, Pawnee and Flathead, Hopi and Zuni—on and on goes the list of the many peoples, each with their unique ways. Each ethnic group filled a niche within the landscape and developed dress, language, beliefs, and behavior that matched their point of view of the world. Some were nomadic and fierce hunters; others gathered roots and berries; others built large permanent towns and cultivated plants and domesticated animals. Hundreds of tribes with diverse language, distinctive modes of survival, and different kinship and religious systems arose in America, and each group had a different history. Evidence of the ancient ones, those who had come before, peoples whose lives and purposes and ultimate fate

were unknown, can be found throughout the land and heard of in the intricate oral history of each group.

Recently a storm in the Northwest Coast pounded away at the shore and when it passed, out of the sand a veritable American Pompeii was revealed. In New Mexico, archeologists dig for the dazzling pottery of the Mimbres culture. So impressive and complex are some archeological areas, such as Chaco Canyon, that it often seems as if the past of this continent and its people must always remain astounding and confounding. Each potsherd unearthed in the excavation of a new sewer line or arrowhead turned up by a farmer's plow offers new proof of their influence.

Much of Native America's effect upon our lives is hidden, despite contributions ranging from the cultivation of corn to the structure of the U.S. Constitution. Our historical view of American Indians is often characterized by extremes—romantic ideals and ethnic stereotypes. Major events in Native American history represent a few lines in American history books, and the relentless American expansionism of the 19th century is clouded by some of our most powerful myths of national identity. What were unknown frontiers to the pioneers were in fact well-known homelands for thousands of Native Americans. Their displacement and in some cases extermination

Above right, a Maricopa tribesman with an exquisite headdress of feathers, late 19th century, and, *below,* elaborately decorated garments of two Blackfeet girls in 1927, are echoes of Native America's past. Canyon de Chelly, Arizona, *below right,* is still a spiritual homeland for the Navajo. Exquisite detail distinguishes the quillwork decoration of the Plains Indian leather bag, *opposite.*

mark a painful and, in the minds of many Native Americans, unresolved period of American history.

During the 19th century tribal groups found themselves either confined to reservations that represented only a small portion of their original homelands or, worse still, moved to entirely different areas and forced to develop new means of subsistence, often under the direct supervision of the U.S. Army. Treaty lands were steadily eroded, sometimes opened up to homesteaders. By the late 19th century, the practices of the settlers and U.S. Government toward the original Americans had shrunk mighty nations to a handful of survivors, as among the Eastern Woodlands people. The highly organized natives of the Southeastern states had been for the most part transferred to reservations in Oklahoma. Nomadic hunters of the Plains and the Far West, such as Navajo and Apache, often fought back, but the widespread slaughter of the buffalo and the dramatic response of the federal government to these activities caused a serious erosion of their populations and eventual demoralization. Indian movement had been almost completely restricted by the turn of the century. Saddest of all of these "Indian affairs" was the fate of the many small hunting and gathering groups that populated the desert areas of the Western states. Dependent upon fragile ecosystems, these small, pacific groups sometimes vanished with little trace—their languages, traditions, and culture irretrievably lost to us all.

The many peoples of the area that became the United States, as well as those in Canada and Mexico, had been set out upon a road from which they could not go back. They had been forced to change; their world no longer belonged exclusively to them. While many predicted the eventual annihilation of the American Indian, a theme common in American literature and visual arts of the late 19th century, Native Americans had no such vision for themselves. They had been here for a long, long time and they meant to be here for a lot longer still.

The traditional arts of Native America were a response to needs within the society. These needs included the demands of the spiritual side of man and even merely functional objects such as bowls, spoons, or combs were often touched by the pervasive influence of the mystic world. In a world in which the gods walked in every forest, swam in every stream, and emerged from the ground and sky, spiritual life invested every act and object with the aura of myth. Human activity was not random, but rather part of a grand and interrelated cosmic scheme. Even the early fishhooks and spoons of Native Americans seem to be imbued with the same force and power as the shaman's rattle or the dance mask. In fact, it is often the functional objects of everyday life that strike us as the most astonishing. The power of an object relates to its expressive and religious nature, not to its status as property. Acquisitiveness and concepts of private property were for the most part imported from the European world. The temptation of wealth in some ways was a lot like smallpox—an invasion against which Native Americans had few defenses.

The collecting of Native American artifacts began as soon as they were discovered, with the curiosities presented by Columbus to the Spanish court. Europe was eager to learn more of this New World.

Responding to the vast range of geographic and climatic conditions in North America, Native Americans developed a variety of housing types, from the elegant and functional dwelling tipi of the Gros Ventre, *top;* the Winnebago lodge of ca. 1889, *center;* and a brush lodge of the Havasupai at Supai Canyon, ca. 1885, *above.* Window Rock, a landmark of the Navajo Reservation, *right,* stands beside yet another type of home—the offices of the tribal administration.

Just as unfamiliar plants and animals were sent to show off the wonders of the new land, so too were people sent—exotic natives with their remarkable dress and ways. Collections were formed in Rome and Madrid, evidence of the first period of contact. It was not until the 19th century, however, that Americans began to collect in earnest the material culture of their own country. Collecting took the form of scientific investigation, including not just objects but ideas—linguistic studies and ethnographic research. By the early 20th century American anthropology had become an important academic field, laying the groundwork for modern perceptions of Native Americans. Artists and photographers came both before and after the anthropologist, at first with scientific, military, and survey groups and later for aesthetic and personal reasons, often capturing a rapidly disappearing style of life. In the wake of the anthropologists and artists came the amateur collectors, who formed the early collections that later served as the bases of the major institutional holdings.

The passion of these early collectors was immense. Unlike other collectors of fine arts, collectors of American Indian arts and artifacts often had to rely upon their own judgment and expertise, developing skills as they went along rather than depending upon art dealers for guidance. The first wave of public interest in collecting Native American art came in the 1960s, fueled by the back-to-the-earth movement and the spiritual questing of this tumultuous period. Native Americans have endured all of these contacts—the anthropologist, collector, and government official—with a benign and wary skepticism.

The continuing interest in Native American arts on the part of the public has been matched not only by a growing community of scholars in the field of Native American studies, but also by a determined and talented group of artists and artisans who have sought to renew, rediscover, and reinvigorate Native arts. Publications, schools, workshops, cooperatives, and annual gatherings and markets have brought the artist community together in a way that was not possible in the past. Communal affiliation and regional identity may no longer be the major concern of the artists, and the functional demands that originally determined the art forms have largely disappeared. Today's artist is limited only by his or her own imagination, the complexity of American Indian mythology, and practical market demands. Despite often harsh conditions, contemporary Native American art and craft displays a great sense of well-being, continuity, and humor.

The unbroken ancestry from the distant past to the present day marks the lives of many contemporary Native Americans. Despite the inevitable losses and breaks from traditional activities and lifestyles, dedicated individuals have maintained, preserved, and passed on the skills and knowledge accumulated over centuries, as well as traditional techniques. What they will pass on to future generations is a legacy as complex, fascinating, and diverse as the many people who developed them over time and space.

A fascinating record of prehistoric concerns can be seen in the petroglyphs at Newspaper Rock, *opposite*. At the turn of the last century, photographer Dana Chase captured on film an Apache named Peso, *above left*. His costume, like the quillwork, *below*, represents the centuries-long traditions of Native America. *Below left*, racers compete at Taos Pueblo on the feast day of San Geronimo, September 30, 1897. The races have been held every year at Taos in late September for centuries.

A young Pueblo woman, Oho-wo-Songwi, from San Ildefonso Pueblo in New Mexico, photographed by Edward S. Curtis in 1905, prepares for a traditional dance by wearing a *tablita* and her finest jewelry.

CLASSICAL TRADITIONS

For thousands of years the Pueblo peoples of the
American Southwest have inhabited the same lands, creating
a continuity of belief, ritual, and artistic traditions.

The importance of religious life among Native Americans is clear not only from the structure of life among recorded and living peoples, but also from the physical and archeological evidence of the past. Reflecting the physical diversity of the land and the many environments it offered is the range of Native American ceremonial customs.

One aspect of this pool of human belief and ritual can be glimpsed in the complex ceremonial cycles of the Pueblo people of the American Southwest. The continuity of human inhabitation among the agricultural Pueblos allowed for the development of an elaborate annual cycle of rituals aimed at assuring the continued abundance and fertility of the land and those who dwelt upon it. Ceremonial structures, such as the circular, semisubterranean kivas, were built to house the ritual and to serve as a visual symbol of the creation of all things by the gods. Rock art or petroglyphs can be found throughout the Southwest, as well as most parts of North America—a tangible reminder that the prehistoric dwellers sought to propitiate their gods and record the important symbols of their religions. Complex symbolism is recorded upon buildings and rocks, woven into fabric, carved upon wood and stone, and drawn upon the landscape itself: nothing escaped the all-pervasive importance and reiteration of ceremony, religion, symbol, and totem.

Despite the differences among the tribes of the Southwest, they share a common environment and a longevity in the region. The demanding ceremonial

Set in the often hostile landscape of the great Southwest, Pueblo Indians evolved decorative yet functional pottery, *above. Above right,* Mariano and Lupita Chavez fashioned traditional moccasins at Cochita Pueblo in New Mexico, in 1920. *Below right,* an early collector, Dr. Logan was able to amass an outstanding collection of baskets from Native Americans living near or around his home in Fort Defiance, Arizona, ca. 1905. The towering rocks of Monument Valley, *opposite,* are the timeless backdrop of the Southwest.

cycle continues despite the time constraints of contemporary life. Some dances, songs, and ceremonies are performed only for the initiated; others are celebrated for all.

At home, Native American women met the eternal tasks of preparing food with the invention of methods and vessels. Among prehistoric and historic groups in the Southwest, women produced great quantities of pottery for use in the preparation and storage of foods. Giant ollas might serve for storing grain or holding water, smaller vessels for boiling meat and beans directly over the fire. Among nomadic groups, pottery yielded to lightweight baskets for storage and food preparation. Large carrying or burden baskets found many uses within the home and served also for transportation of household goods when moving from one area to another. Specially treated baskets could be used to hold water and cook food over a fire. Baskets often played an essential role in the gathering of food.

With the westward expansion of the railroad in the 1880s, the role of both pottery and basketry within many western tribes began to change dramatically. Industrialized products became available for the first time, and utilitarian pots and baskets were seen and purchased for the first time by non-Indians as works of art. This transformation from utility to artwork was to have a profound effect upon these wares as well as on the non-Indians' perception of Native American daily life and cultural achievements.

EARLIEST AMERICAN HOMES

Much of Native American architecture has been lost to the encroachment of American settlers and to the simple passage of time. The portable tipis of the Plains Indians or the fragile elements of the Woodlands wigwams have left little trace upon the landscape, to say nothing of the ancestral pithouses that once dotted the Southwest. What does remain is located largely in the Southwest, both in currently used and inhabited structures and in archeological remains. The many-storied, large, community-based, and interrelated buildings that came to be known as "pueblos" were massive and impressive, and also fairly simple. Constructed of stone masonry or adobe, they were roofed with available wood and grasses and reeds, and plastered inside and out with mud to give a uniform appearance. Ladders were used to gain entry through the roof.

The large, complex pueblo communities of Taos, *above left,* and Jemez, *below left,* in New Mexico were and are still home to farmers whose ancestors have worked the lands for thousands of years. Pueblo communities boast America's oldest continuously inhabited homes.

The Tesuque, *above left*, and Zuni, *below left*, Pueblos are two of nineteen pueblos still in existence today. *Above*, a Buffalo Dancer stands upon a ladder that leads into a kiva, the round, semisubterranean, ceremonial structure that serves as a meeting house.

Chaco Canyon in northwestern New Mexico was the ceremonial heartland of the Anasazi or "ancient ones," whose architectural legacy in the United States is second to none. Complex townscapes included walls of carefully integrated masonry that curved and flowed, *left.* Interrelated doorways, *above,* match the elegance of the exteriors. Once home to thousands, the towns of Chaco were abandoned in the late 13th century.

MUSIC AND DANCE

Ritual reenactment, and tradition are the context that gives meaning to music and dance in Native American life. Regardless of the specific and often subtle meanings conveyed in a dance and its accompanying music, the overall use of both is an intimate reflection of each group's view of life. The sounds in Native American music are close to those produced in nature as opposed to European music with its complex instrumentation, rhythms, and melodies, which move away from the natural world to create a separate aesthetic.

Pueblo dancers, *left*, move to the beat of ceremonial drums, like those from Cochiti Pueblo, *above*. Entering the sacred kiva is one of many parts of the complex and subtle dances, *right*.

Songs could either be personal and popular or ceremonial and sacred. The human voice was the most common instrument, used with words and with "vocables," where the only message was the music itself. The usual accompaniment was percussive—rattles, made of gourds and a wide variety of other materials, including turtle shells and deer hooves—and a variety of skin-covered drums.

Native American dancing is often perceived as aggressive and frenetic, but many dances, as with the examples, *above and right,* from San Ildefonso Pueblo, are quiet and rhythmic.

Young boys, *above left and below,* follow the rhythm and cadence—often as organic and harmoniously repetitive as the beat of the human heart—of the drummers, *below left.*

29

Top, a Butterfly Dancer at San Ildefonso Pueblo in New Mexico wears a tablita made of painted wood, a reflection of the natural world. The Pueblo peoples also incorporated dances and costumes of other groups in their ceremonies, as demonstrated by a Navajo Dance at Cochiti Pueblo in 1920, *above,* and the child with Plains Indian headdress, *right.*

KACHINA

The word "kachina" describes the individual supernatural beings of the spiritual world, the dancers who perform in ceremonies of renewal dressed as kachinas, and the small carved wooden dolls that contain the specific attributes of the deities. When the kachinas come into the Hopi and Zuni villages, they bring with them the promises and protections of the world of the spirit. As the supernatural connectors between the world of the living and the world of the spirit—the upper world and the lower world, the gods and man—the kachinas embody all the many valued aspects of life and the prayer for renewal.

The Hopi world is situated in a desert climate, and each year the hope for renewal comes in the form of a hope for rain and the life that it brings. The kachinas arrive as life begins its renewal in the spring, and they continue their visitations until the promise of new life and moisture show signs of fulfillment. When the Hopi men take on the mask and attributes of the kachina they are to represent, they also adopt the role and the spirit they are about to play. So powerful are the attributes and costume, as well as the role of the kachinas, that many aspects are held in secret so as not to jeopardize the fragile relationship between spiritual and mortal.

The relationship of the dolls made to represent the deities called kachinas, *opposite*, and the mask to be worn by a kachina dancer, *right*, can be seen here. Made from simple materials, in this case saddle leather, the masks take on all of the strength and power of the gods.

One aspect of kachinas, and the one most familiar, is the representation of the kachina in the form of a doll or *tihu*. Given to female children especially, the kachina dolls were gifts in hope of future abundance and health as well as being a tool for the education of the child into the rich and powerful pantheon of the Hopi spiritual world. Originally these figures were flat, unarticulated pieces with only the head and body being distinguishing features. Once the kachina doll became available for sale, first as a curio and later as a work of art, the figures began to evolve into more highly articulated and detailed sculptural pieces. This evolution included the addition of separate attributes to the kachinas such as dance kilts, rattles, sashes, and wands.

At Nedra Matteucci's home in Santa Fe, New Mexico, *opposite,* a collection of kachina dolls fills a part of her study. Both contemporary and 19th-century kachinas are among the most collectible examples of Native American art.

These Hopi pottery tiles representing various kachinas were made in the 1970s by Hopi potters Sadie Adams, Juanita Healing, Lorna Loma Kema, Patricia Honie, Darlene Nampeyo, and non-Hopi artist Rick Dillingham. With more than 250 kachinas in the ever-changing Hopi pantheon, the deities may be male or female, animals or plants, or even abstract concepts.

The development of this type of Hopi tile was the result of early trading and interest in Hopi art shortly before the turn of the century. The trader at Keams Canyon, Arizona, Thomas Keams, was largely responsible for encouraging Hopi potters to produce wares suitable for marketing through the Fred Harvey Company.

The late 19th-century tiles, like the contemporary examples illustrated here, gave the outside world a glimpse of the intricate pantheon of the Hopis. Collector, dealer, and artist Rick Dillingham plays the role of a modern-day Thomas Keams by encouraging innovation and revival among Hopi potter friends. These examples are from his extensive collection.

Few aspects of Hopi artistry have not touched and involved Manfred Susunkewa. A native of Shungopavy at the Hopi Reservation in Arizona, he became involved with traditional crafts in 1959, working with his uncle, noted Hopi jeweler Charles Loloma, in ceramics and jewelry. Susunkewa is also a talented sculptor, painter, and silk-screen artist.

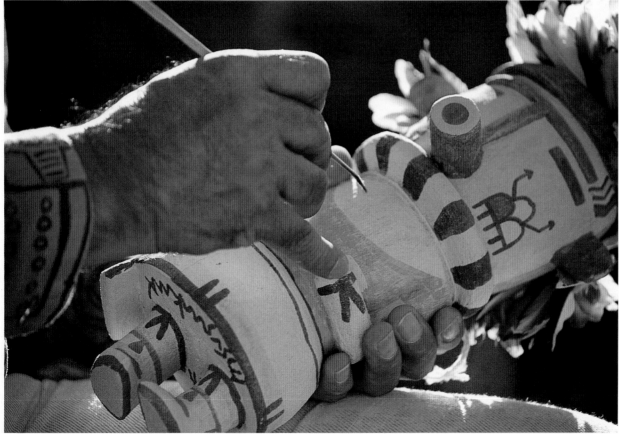

By 1975 Susunkewa had turned to kachinas, which he wanted to re-create in all of their spiritual power and classical form. He spent over a year just collecting materials—cottonwood root for the carving and pulverized clays and rock for the painted decoration. Today he retraces the steps his ancestors took, carving and decorating each kachina by hand.

CLASSIC FORMS

The Pueblo pottery tradition has seen a rapid series of changes in the last 100 years, from decline to curio production, then revival, and finally enormous market success. In large part our appreciation of the contemporary potter's work comes from our growing knowledge and admiration for the work of her ancestors. The prehistoric and historic wares of the Pueblos were of masterful artistry. The beauty of their designs sparked a revival movement in the 1930s, which in turn attracted the attention of Americans and Europeans. The integrity of the early works, with their elegant forms and controlled designs, testifies to the intelligence and complexity of their makers.

Today historic Pueblo pottery, like this classic example owned by Chris Selser, *opposite*, might be displayed with the Hispanic New Mexican pine table and the Navajo wearing blanket. In 1924 Santana Ortiz of Acoma Pueblo illustrated the time-honored use of pottery in the pueblos, the transport and storage of water, *right. Two Zuni Girls at the River* by Edward S. Curtis, *inset right*, dates to the same era.

MIMBRES

From the end of the 13th century to the 19th century the secret of the people of the Mimbres valley lay hidden in the quiet, dry valleys of the unpopulated regions of southwestern New Mexico. An occasional piece of Mimbres pottery surfaced and joined the collection of an officer stationed in the region, but these were regarded as oddities. Not until about 1914 did the revelation occur that beneath the soil was a pictorial record of prehistoric life in the Americas. This record of daily life, of religious attitudes, of beauty and whimsy, was to be found on the concave picture spaces of deep painted bowls.

From A.D. 1000 to 1200 a culture of subsistence farmers produced a special type of pottery, primarily associated with burials, characterized by graphic pictorial representations in black on a white ground. Nearly all of the classic Mimbres black-on-white bowls found in these graves have a hole punched through the bottom after the bowl was decorated and fired. Archeologists surmise that the pots were ceremonially "killed," but there is no conclusive evidence.

What continues to baffle is the incredible attainment of artistry that occurred among these simple folk.

Mimbres potters were highly skilled artisans, so modern scholars assume that the distortion of many of their bowls was purposeful, as in this example, *opposite*. The detail of another example, *right*, depicting a hunter and startled prey, has been "killed"—ritually punctured— as with most Mimbres ware. Further examples, *overleaf*, show the remarkable draftsmanship of the Mimbres potters. Both bowls are in the collection of Dennis and Janis Lyon of Phoenix.

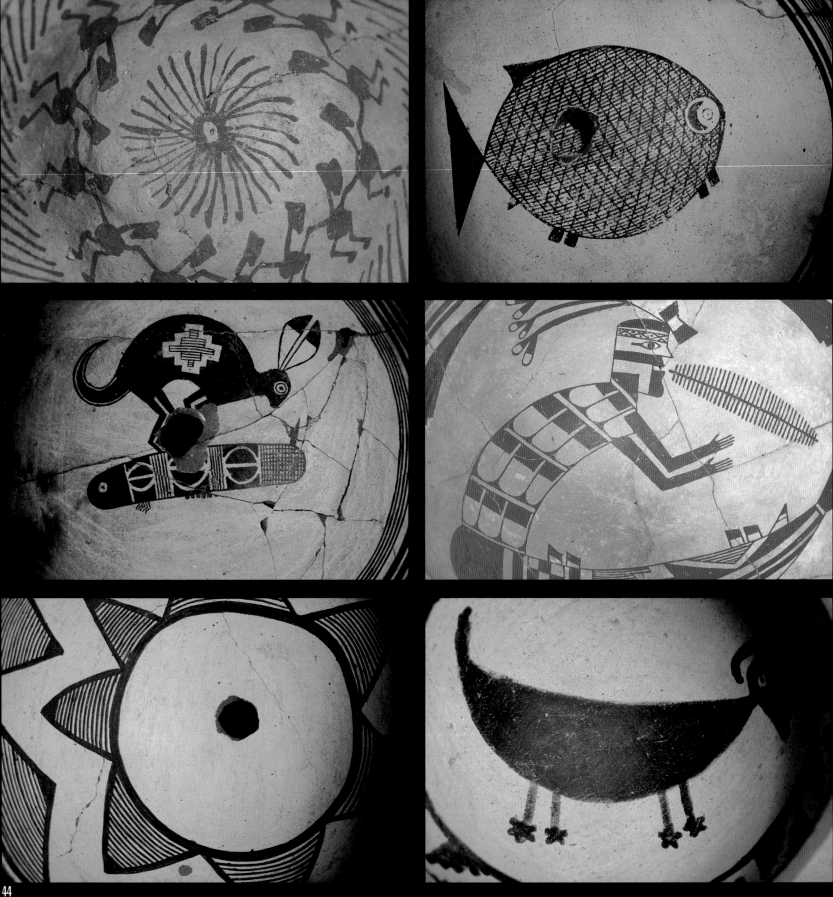

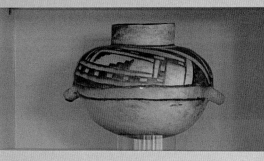

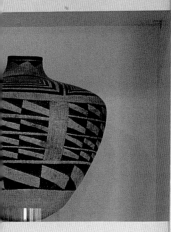

COLLECTION OF CLASSICS

Twelve thousand years ago big game hunters roamed the Southwest tracking mammoths and bison. Gradually, the people of the Archaic Desert Culture cultivated a kind of maize that could be stored, and shortly before Christ the agricultural people today known as the Anasazi settled in villages and increased their numbers, as the production of corn, beans, and squash became more constant and efficient. Like their forebears, the Anasazi traded in turquoise, which found its way far to the south for use by the Aztecs and Toltecs in central Mexico.

Living in the aboveground structures that came to be called pueblos, the Anasazi in many ways set the pattern that would characterize the life of the Southwest to the present day. They used terracing and irrigation to increase productivity, in order to support the large populations that grew in the wake of their successes.

Although much has been pieced together about the Anasazi, there is still more to be learned, especially about their production of pottery. About 80 to 90 percent of the vessels recovered from the Anasazi sites are everyday, utilitarian pieces. The other vessels were painted wares, which give us clues about the aesthetic and skills of these early people. The heyday of this painted pottery, from about A.D. 850 to 1250, opens a window onto these early Native Americans.

Specially built shelves, *left*, house a large and important collection of prehistoric Southwestern pottery. Individual pieces include an unusual large Mimbres olla, *top right*; another olla of a type called Socorro black-and-white (A.D. 1200–1400), *above*; and a large olla, *right*.

PUEBLO POTTERS

Pottery making in the Southwest represents the refinement of a few techniques and materials over many thousands of years. Even the first steps—the selection and preparation of the clay—required great skill and discernment, since it meant long journeys to traditional sites, as well as grinding, winnowing, and mixing of the basic material and its temper. Once the clay was brought to just the right consistency and state of plasticity, it was further kneaded to rid it of air bubbles. There were only two methods of creating pots in Native America—coiling and hand-building. Simple bowls and giant water jars might be created and formed by gradually overlapping coils, each of a uniform width. Once formed, the coils were pressed and scraped into uniformity, allowed to dry, and coated with slip. Then the decoration was either painted or the surface might be incised or polished, and the prepared vessel was fired in a pit using wood or dung. The finished pots provided for the storage, preparation, and cooking of grains and vegetables. They also permitted an avenue of expression that is still an essential part of life of the Pueblo.

Among the Pueblo potters of the 1930s shown at work are, *left,* a Zuni potter painting a geometric design, and *right, clockwise from above right:* a Pueblo potter working on the design of a pot, ca. 1935; a San Juan potter burnishing a large olla, ca. 1935; a Zuni woman adding another coil to the wall of her pot, ca. 1932; and Dolores Vigil at San Ildefonso Pueblo using a yucca leaf as a brush to paint a pot.

A CYCLIC POEM— PUEBLO POTTERY

When the Pueblo potter of New Mexico or Arizona begins her work she reaches back across twenty-four centuries of knowledge. The heaps of potsherds to be sorted at the end of an archeological dig are the broken remnants of this long line of repeated creation. The stories these remnants tell are the distinct perspective of Pueblo life— drought, famine, factionalism, relocation—stories of hardship. These stories are often reflected at the archeological site or in the myth, legend, and reenactments of the people of the pueblos. They might also be reflected in a complex decorative motif painted on a large storage jar, the distillation of centuries of design, in which the representation of a bird or a cloud—a symbol of hope or regeneration— has evolved into a complex geometric pattern. What underlies the many memories of the past is the continual cycle of change, renewal, death, and re-creation.

Gradually, distinctive designs become associated with particular Pueblos. The introduction of mass-produced storage and cookwares at the end of the 19th century required that Pueblo pottery be accommodated to a new audience, a different market. In many cases the remarkable ability of the potter to respond to these new forces led to the creation of revivals of early elegant pottery styles, the development of new decorative styles, and the adaptation of pottery for contemporary American homes.

Until the very recent past all phases of this process—prehistoric, historic, and revival—were regarded as little more than ethnic curiosity or tourist art. Today Pueblo pottery, both past and present, is widely regarded as art.

Historic pottery once served a utilitarian function in every Pueblo household, storing food and water. Today it has become highly sought-after art. This example, *above,* is from the collection of John Kania, Santa Fe, New Mexico.

Two fine examples of historic Pueblo pottery sit on a collector's windowsill, *above.* In the bedroom of collector Richard Howard, *right,* a cupboard full of historic and contemporary pots is flanked by an Anasazi pot and a Tesuque storage jar, ca. 1870. At the far left is a large piece from Santo Domingo Pueblo.

Opposite, one of Richard Howard's most prized pots is a turn-of-the-century Zia Pueblo pot with exquisite painted decoration and a form to match. Throughout Howard's home in Santa Fe, New Mexico, Mexican and New Mexican cupboards house an impressive collection: an early 20th-century pot from Acoma Pueblo and a Zia pot, ca. 1890, *right. Below right,* a Zia pot, early 20th century, and a Cochiti pot, also early 20th century, stand on top of a cupboard over a contemporary Zia pot by Eusabia Shije behind the spindles.

The merging of American traditions occurs in the collection of Robert Nichols and Jonathan Parks. Pottery from Santo Domingo Pueblo is characterized by bold geometry in the ornamentation and a black-and-cream background. Pottery from each New Mexican Pueblo has certain identifiable features in ornamentation, form, and technique. These characteristics became more pronounced over time, and today's potters further emphasize regional variations.

A range of historic pottery fills and tops an American cupboard. Santo Domingo pottery with its distinctive interplay of solids and voids tops the cupboard. Within, the pueblos from A to Z (Acoma to Zuni) are represented. Pueblo pottery has strong and continuous aesthetic ties to the past, with forms and designs from the prehistoric to the present.

Historic Pueblo pottery coexists with Plains Indian beadwork, Navajo and Hispanic textiles, and other traditional and Native American and Hispanic art in this northern New Mexican home, *left and opposite*.

A lifetime of collecting and living with Native American and early Spanish American art is reflected in this interior of a home in northern New Mexico. Spanish textiles and furniture along with Pueblo pottery are the major focus of the collection, accompanied by Plains Indian leatherwork and numerous household implements and decorations of both Spanish and Indian origin.

A comparison of an early interior of a home at Laguna Pueblo, *top*, with a contemporary home, *left*, shows that present-day collectors often take their lead from the past. The natural setting of pottery against adobe walls is a combination that conveys much of the feel of the interiors of the past. A woman coils a pot beside the adobe walls in Zuni Pueblo, *above*.

At the Palace of the Governors in Santa Fe in 1912 photographer Jesse Nusbaum captured the young Maria and Julian Martinez painting and burnishing examples of their pottery. They worked in traditional polychrome style until the late 1920s, but became most famous for their black-on-black style which proved to be immensely popular. Julian died in 1943, but Maria continued to work until her death, by which time she had become the most universally recognized and revered of the Pueblo potters and had revolutionized the making of pottery in her native San Ildefonso. The couple fired pottery in a traditional open-air pit fueled by partially burned dung cakes, *top*. Maria usually made the pots and turned them over to Julian for painting, *above*.

The intricacy and subtlety of classic Martinez pottery is evident in this large olla, *above*. The matte black design against the highly polished black surface, which they perfected in the 1920s, inspired all Pueblo potters to strive for a high degree of virtuosity.

By 1925 Maria Martinez had begun to sign her work. From this grew a new phenomenon that has had an immense effect on the market and on Pueblo pottery: the collecting of the works of known potters. Examples of a collection of Martinez pottery brought together in Phoenix, Arizona, by Dennis and Janis Lyon, *left and right*, illustrates that the collecting of one potter's work can be immensely rewarding.

REVIVAL ON THE MESAS

In 1898 American anthropologist Jesse Walter Fewkes began an archeological investigation of a site that was ancestral to the Hopi Indians of Arizona. The clues uncovered by this dig were to launch a new phase in the development of Hopi craft. What Fewkes discovered was nothing less than one of the high points in the creation and decoration of pottery in the New World. While related to what had come before, the pots from this site were clearly products of an artistic explosion. Their virtuosity and brilliant decoration were quite beyond anything that had been seen before.

One of the workers at the site was a young Hopi man named Lesou; his wife was a young potter from Tewa Village (Hano) named Nampeyo. Lesou shared with Nampeyo shards that bore the brilliant black-on-orange designs of this classic pottery. From her introduction to the Sikyatki Polychrome pottery—so named by Fewkes after the First Mesa prehistoric town—Nampeyo developed a neo-Classic style of pottery that came to be called Sikyatki Revival. She brought back to Hopi pottery the elegance and brilliance of a previous period, restyling her pots in the image of what had come before and re-creating the complex and sophisticated designs of the black-on-orange designs and the black-on-yellow wares that had followed.

Interestingly, this rediscovery of the Classic phase of Hopi life came at about the same time that the Hopi mesas were being opened up to influences from the outside world. From the time of the Pueblo Revolt in the late 17th century until the final years of the 19th, Hopis were able to live in splendid isolation from the European and American life that had invaded and damaged so many other Native American groups in the last century. The greatest threat during these centuries was not from the missionaries and soldiers, which had disrupted other Native American lifeways, but rather from other Indian groups, most notably the Navajos. As a

On the table, *left,* are contemporary Hopi pots made by the relatives of the Hopi potter Nampeyo. Nampeyo's descendants continue to work in the low-shouldered shapes of prehistoric Hopi pottery, which she revived with the help of her husband, Lesou. *Above right,* a contemporary Hopi pot is safely displayed on top of a blue cupboard in the home of the Hopi painter Dan Namingha, another of Nampeyo's descendants.

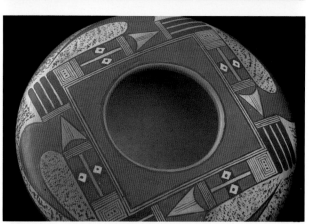

result the Hopis were free to continue to pursue their complex ceremonial and social life without interruption, despite Navajo pressures. When the missionaries finally came, the anthropologists and Indian agents followed quickly on their heels. The ethnologists were able to observe Native American culture intact—an uninterrupted panorama from prehistory to the present. They also bore witness to a culture in the throes of change. From 1890 to 1940, a short fifty years of Hopi history, they were to face all of the many invasive, disruptive, and destructive elements of the outside world.

Nampeyo was very much a part of this world in transition. Her fame as a potter was to make Hopi a destination for those seeking fine examples of Native American craft. On a number of occasions she and her family left Hopi so that they could demonstrate pottery, particularly at the newly created Hopi House at the Grand Canyon. She was the subject of a number of photographic studies; most memorable are those by A. C. Vroman and Edward S. Curtis, which produced for the rest of the world a vision of the timelessness of Hopi culture.

The Hopi revival pottery, *left*, is from the collection of Rick Dillingham. *Right*, classic Hopi pottery served as the inspiration for the revival movement of the late 19th and early 20th centuries (collection of Dennis and Janis Lyon, Phoenix).

MARY LEWIS
ACOMA
POTTER

After she had seen all eight of her children settled in school, Mary Lewis decided that the time had come to learn from her mother, famed Acoma ceramicist Lucy Lewis, the time-honored traditions of the Acoma potters of New Mexico. She began first with miniatures, a size she still enjoys, and gradually began coiling larger and larger pots. At first her mother outlined the design with a yucca brush and Mary filled it in, but soon she created her own pots, from the digging of the clay to the firing in an open pit fueled with dung.

Painting a pot, *above,* requires intense concentration and patience, to say nothing of years of practice and skill. Practice and talent are evident in Mary Lewis's exquisite final products, *above right,* and the care with which she assembles the raw materials, *right.*

Mary's sense of design grew from studying her mother's work, examining historic Acoma pottery, and searching for the roots of Acoma design through the study of pottery from Mimbres, Chaco Canyon, and Mesa Verde (Colorado) prehistoric painted wares. She maintains her focus on the tradition, using only native clay and mineral paints. Lewis's siblings are also potters, and Mary is passing her skills on to her children.

Mary Lewis, *above*, has good reason to be proud of her work, the legacy of prehistoric, historic, and contemporary Pueblo potters. The potter's tools have remained essentially the same over the centuries, *right;* family tradition steers Lewis to suitable clays and minerals; yucca leaves serve as brushes.

INDIAN MARKET

When Dr. Edgar Lee Hewett outlined his proposal for a market in Santa Fe, New Mexico, in 1922, he clearly never dreamed that it would achieve so brilliantly the goal which he established. "It is not expected that the initial effort will be productive of anything spectacular, either in quality or dimension," he stated, "but it is sincerely hoped and believed that the beginning thus made will result in future exhibitions of the greatest value to all classes of citizens, particularly to the Indian."

Santa Fe seldom slumbers anymore, but when the week of Indian Market arrives it positively explodes into a buying frenzy of Native American art. Even before the light of day has cracked over the Cathedral, the Plaza is full of expectant buyers and sellers. By five A.M. lines have formed by a few of the booths, lines of buyers hoping to have a chance to buy directly from the maker the Best of Show or one piece of a small but select output from a famous artist. With all of this excitement and expectation that the current market engenders, it is hard to imagine that the earliest market was a modest and humble proposal to encourage the few remaining crafts-people in the Santa Fe area.

Thousands crowd the Indian Market each August in Santa Fe, *left,* swelling the year-round population. The variety of size, scale, quality, and artistry available at Indian Market can seem overwhelming. Pottery predominates among the crafts, but shell, quill, and beaded necklaces, silver jewelry, and baskets are also displayed, *opposite.*

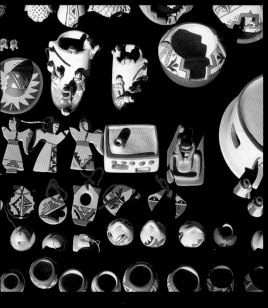
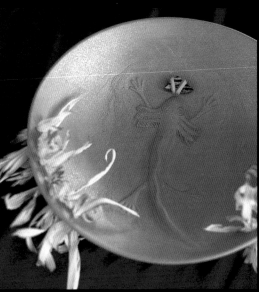

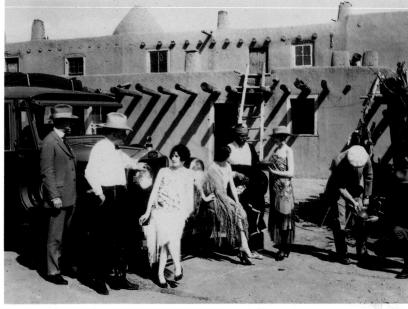

Left, the Palace of Governors' portal, Santa Fe, served as one of the early markets for the purchase of Pueblo pottery, as seen here in 1935. This practice followed the first Indian markets and was instituted to give encouragement to native craftspeople. The Indian Detour buses run by the Fred Harvey Company, *top and above,* were part of a commercially run venture to introduce tourists to Native Americans by taking them directly to the pueblos.

American basketry reached its zenith in the late 19th century, as seen in these fine examples of Chemehuevi baskets displayed by their maker in Southern California. Master basket makers were first recognized by name during this era, and their works were purchased by non-Indians for their artistry.

BASKETS— EPHEMERAL ARTISTRY

The making of baskets for the storage, preparation, and gathering of food preceded the development of pottery making in the New World by many centuries and required highly developed skills and a knowledge of the land. Plaiting, coiling, and twining, not to mention harvesting and preparation of materials, are skills demanding great dexterity.

Despite these demands, the art of basket making achieved an extraordinarily high level in many areas of North America. In California, for example, a large number of native groups fostered the development of basketry; the Pomo, Yurok, Hupa, and Chemehuevi all produced fine baskets. In California as well as the Southwest and Northwest Coast, baskets not only played a practical role, but were a common accompaniment to ceremony, sometimes as headgear, sometimes as props for ceremonial dances. Among Hopis of the Southwest, flat wickerwork baskets held cornmeal and *pikki* bread; similar shapes with special designs and patterns were offered as gifts at ceremonies and used in the women's Basket Dance.

For the most part, basket making is women's work. Like pottery and weaving, basketry became an important expressive medium, and many women achieved innovation, creativity, and aesthetic excellence. This striving and perfection can be clearly seen in the works of both the known and anonymous makers. The great technical and artistic demands of the craft were in many ways also its undoing. Of all the Native arts in North America, none was greater than that of basket making, but no craft suffered more from the dislocations of the 19th century. The immediate effect of a monied economy and a market for the sale of baskets was liberating, and produced some of the greatest works in the 19th century, but as the functional use for baskets disappeared, so did the necessity for passing on the craft.

Large flat baskets, such as this one held by a young woman from Isleta Pueblo, New Mexico, ca. 1890, were especially used for the washing of wind-winnowed wheat in a moving stream. Once clean, the wheat was left to dry in large flat baskets.

Apaches were particularly adept basket makers and contributed a number of elegant forms and fascinating designs. Besides large ollas, Apaches regularly made small, handsome jars, which were then lined with melted pine pitch to make them watertight. Large conical burden baskets, for hauling wood, food, and other household commodities, are much sought after by the contemporary collector. The designs on Apache baskets include figures of deer, men, horses, and dogs, as well as geometric designs and stylized floral patterns. From about 1880 to 1940, the time of the first reservation until World War II, basketry among the Apaches was remarkably prolific, technically superior, and innovative. An outstanding collection of Western Apache ollas in an Arizona collection, in the left corner an example of Pima basketry with a fretwork design, all from ca. 1900–1930.

The Native Americans of New England have been making large, utilitarian splint baskets for centuries. During colonial times and later, itinerant male basket makers traveled from village to village, carrying their wares on their backs, a practice that greatly served the New England householder, Indian and non-Indian alike. Pack baskets, laundry baskets, and sewing baskets were but a few of the types sold. Some had modest painted or stamped designs or alternating bands of color.

The collector of the baskets on these pages has examples of not only the large splint baskets, but also fancy baskets made by Native American women in the late 1800s. Fancy baskets were usually more whimsical and inventive than their utilitarian counterparts and could include such playful items as dollhouse furniture, glove boxes, trinket boxes, and charming little strawberries. Twists, curls, and imported paper twine dressed up their surfaces.

Another favored medium of the Eastern Woodlands basket maker was birchbark, which was shaped into a variety of forms and decorated with scratched-in pictographs of human and animal life and decorative designs.

From along the waterways of Louisiana comes the cane used by the Chitimacha people of the Southeastern United States to fashion elegant and often quite subtle baskets. After the cane was cut and dyed with black walnut and dock plant, the baskets were made entirely without the use of any tools. Their designs are generations old and bear such names as "eye of cattle," "mouse tracks," and "turtle with a necktie." To pass on the complex designs, the basket makers save a basket as a model. If the sample is sold, the design is lost. Baskets were made in a variety of forms to meet such functional needs as winnowing and storage. Little heart-shaped baskets were hung on the wall as pockets for small household objects. There are very few Chitimacha left and even fewer basket makers.

COLLECTING AN ANCIENT ART

Because the materials used in the creation of baskets are so ephemeral, few clues remain to suggest how this craft developed in Native America. Only the basket makers' creations remain as testimony to their achievement.

Like many who become fascinated with an aspect of Native America, Natalie Linn quickly discovered that she would have to nourish her interest by becoming not just a collector, but also a scholar and later a dealer—in order to upgrade her collection and share the expertise that she had acquired. Today she is surrounded by Native American basketry, particularly the coastal and inland arts of her home state, Oregon, and the creations of neighboring California and the Northwest Coast of Canada. Like the collector of a fine art, she was sought to acquire the finest examples and then learn as much as possible about the circumstances surrounding the creation and its maker.

Top left, Tlingit rattle-top baskets from southeast Alaska are finely woven of spruce root, bear grass, and maidenhair fern, ca. 1890–1920. *Center left,* a Chehalis cylindrical basket combines figures and symbols. *Left,* a series by Mary Moses, Nootka, British Columbia, ca. 1970–1985, are small treasury baskets of dyed and natural bear grass. *Right,* two Wasco baskets from Oregon, 1880–1890, of hemp, cattail, cornhusk, and hide, were used to gather roots. Nez Percé cornhusk bags are the backdrop for all of the baskets on these two pages.

The finely twined cornhusk bags from the Plateau became an important vehicle for expression among the Nez Percé around the turn of the 20th century. The technique required fierce concentration, but offered the opportunity for individual creative expression: the images on each side are almost always different. At the turn of the century, access to aniline dyes and aniline-dyed fibers gave the weavers a new range of colors, which they explored with a sense of verve. Their new choice of colors gave impetus to the repertoire, and weavers introduced pictorial motifs in response to changes in their lives.

BASKET MAKERS

The techniques of basket making —coiling, plaiting, and twining— were employed throughout Native America with infinite variety. Not only did the makers show skill and inventiveness in the weaving of the baskets, but they also used a range of materials in ingenious ways. In the Southwest, some of the most proficient basket makers were the Apaches, whose repertoire included twined baskets, cone-shaped burden baskets, globular water-jar baskets with a waterproofing layer of pine pitch, and coiled baskets. The many hunting and gathering peoples of California also produced some of the most elegant and sophisticated designs ever achieved in the weaving arts.

One of the most ancient crafts of the Americas, basket making was practiced among many groups, by both men and women, for utilitarian and ceremonial needs, and with various techniques and degrees of proficiency. *From top left, clockwise,* are basket makers at Jemez, Hopi, and San Ildefonso Pueblo, and a Diequeño from California. *Right,* a Hopi basket maker sits before a traditional pueblo, ca. 1901.

The gathering of plant materials was a pre-dominant activity among almost all Native American groups; for the basket maker it was a crucial prelude to her craft, and often required every bit as much time and skill as the weaving. An elder from the Cherokee tribe, *above,* demonstrates her skill at a tribally run "living" museum in Tahlequah, Oklahoma. Grasses and other plants, *right,* form an attractive display: *from left to right,* Cholla wood, Indian rice grass, Navajo tea (cota), snake broom, chamisa blanco, Wright's buckwheat, panic grass, and yerba del Manso.

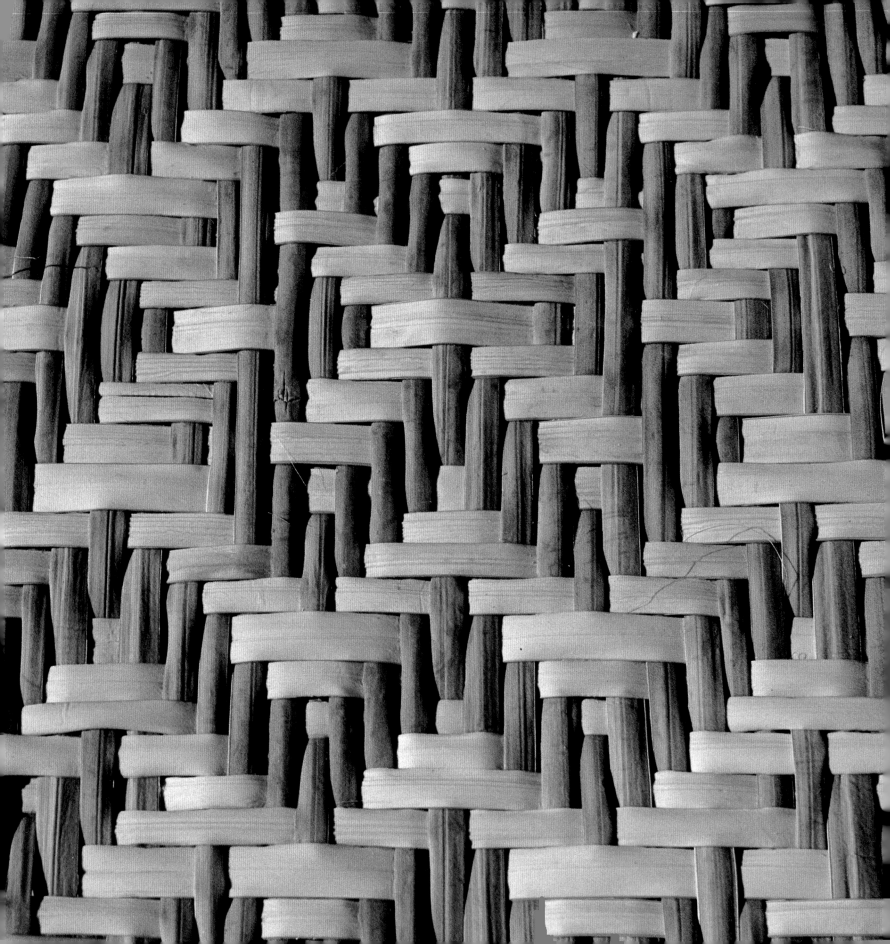

FERMINA BANYACYA — BASKET MAKER

All of her life Fermina Banyacya has lived and worked on the Hopi reservation at Kykotsmovi in Arizona. Her mother, a talented and well-known basket maker, wanted her daughter to carry on the family tradition, which had spanned at least four generations. In the 1950s Fermina learned her mother's art. She now passes on her basket-weaving skills through adult education classes on the reservation.

Banyacya's first step in making a basket is to gather yucca, which she does all year; winter months, when the leaves are pliable, are best. After gathering, the fiber must be stripped and split. Wide strips serve best for the woven baskets and plaques; the smaller strips are used for the coiled baskets. From the basic diamond-shaped design she fashions her own distinctive patterns, expressing creativity within the tradition.

With plain and twill plaiting, the basket maker can achieve a variety of geometric patterns such as zigzags, chevrons, and diagonals, seen in the detail of Fermina Banyacya's work, *left*, and a finished basket, *above*. In this technique, Banyacya plaits first, *right*, then attaches the piece to a frame.

STAFF OF LIFE

The contribution of Native Americans to the cooking pots of the world is immeasurable. Imagine a world without tomatoes, potatoes, chile, or chocolate. Thanks to the cultivation of plants and domestication of animals in the New World, the menus of the Old World were transformed.

Of all the foods developed among Native Americans perhaps the greatest was corn. It was grown in countless varieties and formed the staple of diets throughout the New World. Honoring that role, Native

Left, above, and right: By the time that Columbus made his first sighting of cornfields in 1493, the farmers that had been here before him had developed about 200 to 300 varieties of corn. These early farmers often bred for color and developed the yellow, white, blue, red, black, and multicolor hues now referred to as "Indian corn." From Colonial times to the present day, this hard corn has been popularly used for popcorn.

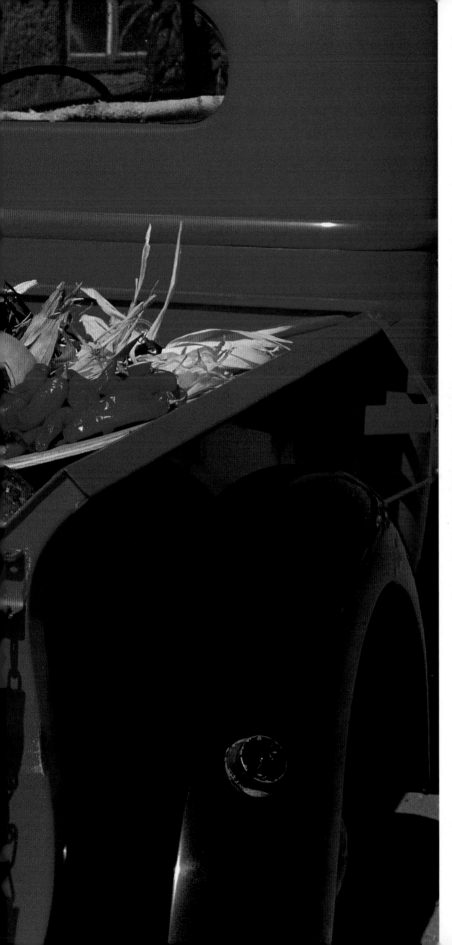

Americans paid homage to corn with images and ceremonies.

The gathering, hunting, and harvesting of food involved every member of every tribal group in North America, regardless of habitat. Through scrutiny of the landscape, careful husbandry, sensitivity to nature, and ingenuity, the peoples of the New World developed an intimate knowledge of the environment. Many tribal groups followed a seasonal cycle of hunting and gathering, moving in their proscribed territories and harvesting seasonally, sometimes supplementing gathering with agriculture. Beyond the simple harvesting of nature's bounty for food, clothing, medicines, and even poisons, some groups cultivated

crops, particularly the Indian triad: beans, squash, and corn.

The streams, lakes, and oceans, plains, mountains, and deserts yielded fish and game. Gradually, Native America created a rich and diverse cuisine, which enriched the repertoire of Europe when it was discovered. Such American institutions as clambakes, barbecues, corn bread, and pumpkin pie are the result of New World foods, sometimes in combination with Old World techniques of preparation.

Among the Indian fruits, vegetables, and nuts were cactus, piñon nuts, acorns, wild berries, and greens. Although these have largely been superseded by agricultural products, native fish and game, such as smoked salmon, lobster, and oysters, have become some of our favorite delicacies.

The ancestors of Native Americans cultivated several kinds of crops, including the Indian corn, *top,* **and pumpkins in the back of a pickup truck in the Southwest,** *left.* **Women at Zuni Pueblo plant corn in a traditional waffle garden,** *above.*

The annual Indian Market in Santa Fe, *above,* is a good place to sample such traditional fare as Navajo fry bread, *top,* along with the Tex-Mex combinations that have become part of the Native American diet. A monument photographed at the beginning of the 20th century, *right,* leaves no doubt that corn is king. The Apaches and other corn lovers were recorded at a Corn Show.

Photographed by Ben Wittick in the studio in 1882 and identified as "Navajo Buck," this young Navajo faces his nation's changing future, posed with a rifle in his hands.

JOURNEY TO CHANGE

Facing overwhelming challenges to their survival,
the Navajo have not only adapted to change, but have created a unique and
lasting culture celebrating age-old traditions and modern technologies.

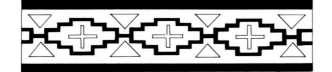

In 1882 frontier photographer Ben Wittick captured forever the tough integrity of a Navajo scout, Chich-Is-Nez, *above.* The landscape of the Navajo reservation has changed little since the late 19th century. A few Navajo still return each summer to their ancestral home, the Canyon de Chelly, *right,* while others graze their sheep in the open range of the reservation, *opposite.*

Within the boundaries of the United States sits another nation. It extends for hundreds of miles and encompasses landscape that for many summarizes the American West—open, undeveloped, harsh, dramatic, and compelling. Despite its seeming emptiness this nation is populated by the largest single Native American tribe—the Navajos. They share proximity and territory with other groups, primarily the Hopi and Zuni, a source of dispute for many. Linguistically, their origins lie far to the north, among Athapaskan speakers, suggesting that the nomadic Navajo came to the Southwest long after their agriculturally dependent neighbors, the Pueblo Indians. That this nomadic people should be settled upon the largest sovereign reservation and have the greatest numbers of members is a remarkable story of endurance and adaptability. The story of the Navajo includes a bitter transition from a nomadic and semiagrarian lifestyle to forced settlement, a period marked by armed conflict, forced migration, starvation, and disease.

Long before the white man arrived here in the 16th century, these Apachean people had begun to adapt to some of the ways of their Pueblo neighbors. Although they continued to live in semi-isolation in loose clans rather than the tight, cohesive towns and communities of the Pueblos, they began cultivating corn and adopted some Pueblo religious practices. With the coming of the Spaniards to the Southwest and with them the introduction of horses and sheep, the pattern of adaptation and integration of new technologies became firmly established among the Navajo. With the Spanish came not only the sheep but the entire cultural history of Europe, the Middle East, and North Africa. Although influences both in technology and design can be traced in the history of development of the Navajo blanket, at some level there is no accounting for the tremendous creativity, integrity, and energy that emerged in this process. The Navajo succeeded not only in mastering technique but also in integrating technological innovations, new designs, and cultural influences in a way that could be recognized and admired by people of very diverse backgrounds.

By the late 19th century the steady incursions of the Navajo warriors upon Pueblo, Spanish, and Anglo-Americans incurred a response that nearly decimated the tribe. The U.S. Army confined the Navajos in the Bosque Redondo on the Pecos River, reducing their numbers to just 8,000 and making necessary the restructuring of their tribal life. The years following the incarceration at Bosque Redondo were to see the development of the craft of silversmithing among the Navajo, a craft learned from the Spanish sometime between 1850 and 1870. Once rooted within Navajo culture, the practice quickly spread to other tribal groups in the area, especially at Zuni, Isleta, Hopi, and to the northern Pueblos. In this case the Navajos did the sharing of the knowledge, but they maintained a devoted interest in the craft. Even today jewelry is an important commodity of Navajo life.

The Navajos rebuilt their community within the reservation system. There the trader and trading post, the Bureau of Indian Affairs, the railroad, and the tourist eventually had an enormous effect, but the Navajos survived these vicissitudes to triumph in their arts, bringing the crafts of weaving and silversmithing to new levels of excellence.

WEB OF TRADITION

Of all the technologies that the Navajo were to add to their repertoire, the art of weaving—first developed by Puebloan people over the centuries—was to have the most profound effect upon their destiny and upon their expressive powers. The cotton and later the wool that the Hopis and other Pueblo Indians fashioned into mantas and other wearing and utilitarian fabrics became important commodities in the Southwest. The Spanish exploited textiles in their efforts to establish an economic base in the region. By the 18th century, Navajos had become proficient weavers and sheep raisers. When the Anglo-Americans came upon the scene in the mid-19th century, the Navajo blanket, woven by women, was already highly prized, admired not only for the fineness of the weave but also for its compact and compelling sense of design.

While the Puebloan peoples were agriculturalist—planting and harvesting the cotton used in their textiles—the Navajos for the most part maintained their nomadic ways, becoming instead herders of the sheep from which they derived

The contemporary pictorial rug, *left,* is made by Navajo women on the traditional upright loom. Navajo women, *above right, above far right, and below right,* learned the art of spinning and weaving from their Puebloan neighbors, such as Hopi men, *below far right.*

the raw material of their developing craft. Forever the raiders and warriors, Navajo males thrived in the vast and demanding terrain of the American Southwest. Harassing Spanish and Pueblo villages alike, they helped themselves to horses, guns, food, and women when the opportunity arose, and as a result often became the focus of punitive military actions on the part of their victims. Despite this behavior, the Spanish greatly admired the Navajos' skill and industry, particularly their weavings. The adaptive propensities of the weavers extended not only to the adoption of new technologies, but most especially to the integration of new motifs and designs into an ever-expanding repertoire.

Today Navajo weaving is still a family affair. Isabel John, *above far left,* has handed down the tradition of pictorial weaving to her daughter, Geanita John, who in turn is beginning to teach her daughter, Angelita, *below left.* Mae Jim of Ganado, Arizona, works on a rug of heroic proportions, *right,* which took twenty-seven months to weave, following three months for the preparation of the wool.

The magnificent mountains outside of Taos, New Mexico, serve as the setting for Classic period Navajo wearing blankets from the collection of artist Jack Silverman. These early weavings from his collection serve as the direct models for his stunningly realistic serigraphs of Southwestern textiles. This graphic art makes these rare textiles available to those who might otherwise have little opportunity to experience their beauty.

RAMONA SAKIESTEWA —HOPI WEAVER

The Santa Fe, New Mexico weaver, Ramona Sakiestewa combines traditional techniques with her own interpretive style to create unique contemporary textiles that capture the colors and forms of the Southwest. Like many Native Americans she explores the culture of her ancestors through her art, as well as her own past. Sakiestewa mastered the vertical loom techniques that were originally the legacy of Pueblo weavers and then learned to weave on the treadle loom. Through her art she has bridged the Anglo world of her youth with the Hopi world of her ancestry. Her sense of commitment to these two communities is represented not only in her art, but also in her willingness to serve—she is a member of the board of the New Mexico Arts Commission—as a tireless advocate of Native values and individual visions.

At her workshop off Garcia Street in Santa Fe, Ramona Sakiestewa combines traditional designs with contemporary themes and technology to produce a personal art.

111

SOLID GEOMETRY

Navajo blanket styles reveal the stages of development and current events in the group itself. The earliest period, which includes First Phase and Second Phase Chief's blankets along with serape-style textiles, extends from about 1800 to 1870. During this period all of the Classic features of the Navajo blanket were realized. The common denominator of the textiles, bands and/or stripes, were used in an innovative and self-assured manner; the colors, although often natural or vegetal, were bold; and they were tightly and neatly woven. Navajo textiles distinguished themselves in the fine points of design and composition: blocks of color in the corners, variegation of the yarn, and variation in the widths of the bands and stripes. An intense interplay of color heightened the dynamic quality and textural interest of the basic composition. So great was their concern for color that when the brilliant scarlet of a commercial fabric called "bayeta" was introduced, Navajo women unraveled the fabric in order to incorporate it into Navajo blankets. When synthetic dyes and commercially dyed and spun yarns from Germantown, Pennsylvania, were introduced, the Navajo weavers unhesitatingly—and unerringly—leaped into the world of color.

Traditional weavings such as this Child's Blanket from the collection of Charles and Sharon Aberle, *left,* serve as inspirations for contemporary weavings such as those at the collection, *right,* of the Cameron Trading Post in Arizona, which include, *clockwise from top left:* a detailed geometric by Marilyn Roan of Wide Ruins; a Third Phase Chief's blanket; a blanket in a traditional design of interlocking diamonds; a Third Phase transitional blanket; a copy of an early textile by Stella Begay of Cameron, Arizona; and a Ganado red blanket.

The bold design of the Wedge-Weave Style blanket, *left*, was executed in the last years of the 19th century. The use of red, white, and blue as well as other patriotic motifs can be found throughout Native American art, from textiles to beaded bags. In the case of the Navajos, it has been supposed that the colors and composition of the American flag appealed to their sense of design, since it strongly resembles the Navajo Chief's blanket.

The remains of a Navajo rug now cover the seat of this Mexican Colonial-styled chair. On the floor is a Navajo rug. Traders on the reservation not only made commercial products available to the weavers but also began to tailor the Navajo textiles as a viable commercial commodity to be sold to Anglo-American customers. It was at this point that Navajo textiles changed from utilitarian wearing blankets to rugs, and the primary users from Native Americans to the American public.

Robert Nichols of Santa Fe, New Mexico, has fused his interests in American folk art with that of his collecting in the field of Native American art. *Above,* a hooked rug and a Pueblo textile hang on the bedroom walls; a Pendleton blanket and a Navajo blanket cover the bed and chair. Part of his extensive collection of Pueblo pottery is upon the bureau.

Left, the Santa Fe home of art dealer and collector Jordan Davis is a showcase for fine Navajo blankets and classic historic Pueblo pottery. The home of Lane and Jane Coulter, *right,* reflects a lifetime of assembling a fine Native American art collection, which features many important Navajo textiles.

Among the textiles in the Durango Collection, formed in Durango, Colorado, by Mark Winter and Jackson Clark, are an exquisite series of Navajo child's wearing blankets, hung in Winter's office, which is also home to basketry from Arizona and California and an ever-expanding collection of Indian kitsch, *left.* In Winter's living room, *right,* a Hispanic Rio Grande textile on the wall complements a Germantown Eyedazzler Navajo textile on the floor. Plains Indian moccasins line up just beneath the roof beams. *Below right,* the Channing-Dale-Throckmorton gallery in Santa Fe, New Mexico, displays another important aspect of Navajo textile design—the Yei (Navajo Holy People) rug, a type of weaving developed at the beginning of the 20th century.

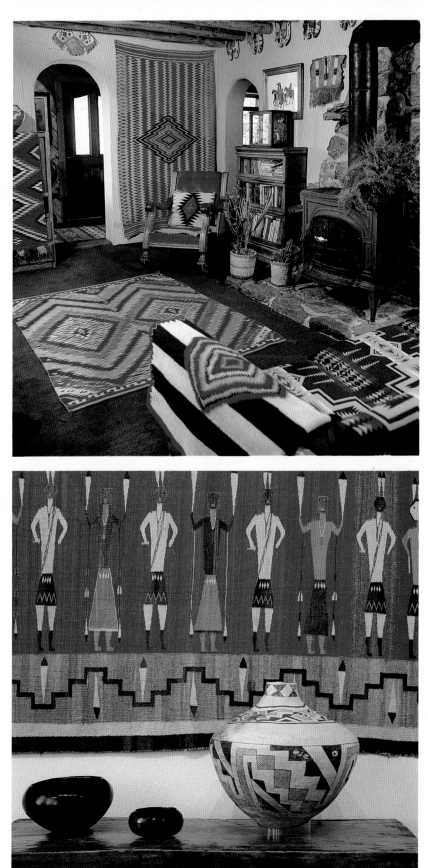

PICTORIAL REFERENCES

Today's Navajo pictorial rugs are part of a tradition that began in the mid-19th century. Weavers began adding small pictorial motifs, such as animals and men, to their otherwise geometric textiles. By the late 19th century the impact of life on the reservation had given rise to pictorial motifs that ranged from woven lettering to American flags and other patriotic symbols.

Now as then, pictorial rugs represent only a tiny fraction of the textiles produced by the Navajos, but they continue to reflect influences and changes.

Bouncing rabbits and pecking hens are the serialized motifs of the pictorial rug, *above far left*. Rows of animal motifs appear in the earliest pictorial rugs. Fannie Mann and her son, *above left*, hold up one example of her many large rugs, which show her perceptions of life on the Navajo reservation, a world that includes traditional water tanks, windmills, hogans, and cattle, as well as a 7-Up sign and a gas station. *Left*, the flag rug by weaver Mae Henio was offered at the periodic rug auction in Crownpoint, New Mexico.

Weaver Fannie Mann proudly displays a reservation-scene rug in front of her pickup truck—the predominant mode of transportation on the reservation, *left.* Pictorial rugs reflect a wide variety of sentiments, including a cheery "Welcome," *top.* A small and early sample of Fannie Mann's work, *above,* is in the collection of Christine and Davis Mather, Santa Fe.

PENDLETON BLANKETS

During the last years of the 19th century the Pendleton Woolen Mills of Pendleton, Oregon, began making woolen blankets for a unique clientele—Native Americans, specifically the Nez Percé and Umatilla, who had a strong and active presence near the mill. These industrially produced wearing blankets had pan-Indian motifs and colors that the mill's designers hoped would appeal to their Native American customers. Appeal they did, not only to the local tribes but to Native Americans throughout the country and to non-Indians as well. By the first decades of the 20th century the company was producing attractive color catalogues featuring everything from blankets and shawls to bathrobes—all done in Indian-style motifs—with the promise of free delivery anywhere in the United States.

Like the blankets manufactured by the Hudson's Bay Company of Canada, the Pendletons had a

Pendleton blankets were the wearing blankets of choice back in 1935 at San Juan Pueblo, New Mexico, when these photos were taken by T. Harmon Parkhurst. Among Native groups the Pendleton blanket became synonymous with quality, and substitutes were not accepted.

distinctive appeal first as an important trade item and later as a status symbol. The number of blankets owned was a measure of wealth among Native Americans, who appreciated their high quality. The fabric was—and is—woven of the finest wools so closely that it keeps out the wind and is virtually waterproof, as well as lightweight and extremely durable. Even after laundering, the original colors are preserved, and the fibers endure the hardest wear. While other blanket companies made products with Indian motifs, none achieved Pendleton's level of quality. Today only Pendleton survives as a maker of fine Indian-motif blankets, which are often the preferred gift for births and marriages, and are even used as shrouds for Native American burials.

Many of the elements of Western Americana are brought together in this quiet bedroom in Santa Fe, *left.* Despite the many color and pattern variations of the Pendleton blankets on the beds, they always seem to work together well. Many of the newly made blankets, *top and above,* have the same color schemes of greens and browns as the originals.

In the history of the Pendleton company more than 200 designs were developed, of which a scant 14 are available today—but in more than 20 color combinations. Early Pendletons had simple stripes, blocks, rectangles, and crosses. Advances in textile manufacturing, primarily through the introduction of the Jacquard loom, allowed designers to experiment with intricate geometric designs.

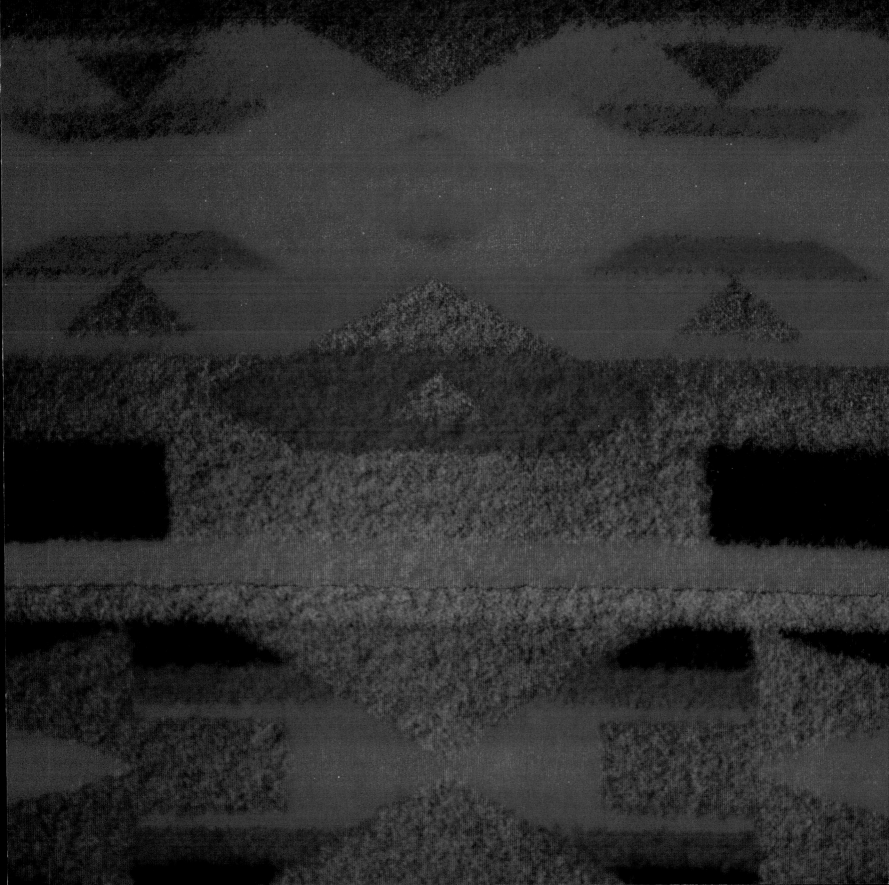

Crow Fair, held annually at the Crow Indian reservation in Montana, features a number of parades. In one of the most impressive, families decorate their cars with beautiful textiles such as Pendleton blankets and embroidered shawls, so that those dressed in their finest regalia can be carried on these wonderful improvised "floats." One little girl, *top*, has had enough excitement for one day. Another truck, *above*, trails its finery both front and back.

A beautiful young Crow woman, adorned in her finest, stands in front of a well-dressed car, *right*. During the parade she rode on the hood of the car while it moved slowly through the encampment.

Juanita, the wife of Navajo chief Manuelito, is seen surrounded by some of the most important signs of wealth among her people—blankets and silver jewelry.

WEALTH OF A NATION

The two major crafts of the Navajo, weaving and silversmithing, have become emblematic of the contribution Native Americans have made to American art. This is especially interesting in the case of silversmithing, since the first Navajo silverwork dates only to about the 1850s. It was not until after the incarceration at Bosque Redondo of 1863–1868 that silver jewelry became a focus of importance.

Introduced by the Spanish, first to Navajo smiths and not much later to the nearby Pueblos, the craft spread quickly. Soon the possession of both the knowledge and the product had become entrenched in the culture of the Southwest. In the 1890s the setting of turquoise in silver began, and the importance of the newly created jewelry was ensured. Not long afterward the opening of the railroads brought tourists, widening silver's significance to far beyond the reservation.

The Pueblo Indian woman, *right,* wears very similar jewelry. The interchange between Navajo and Pueblo was always great in the course of the history of jewelry development in the Southwest and an exchange between the groups remains significant to the present day.

As with weavings, the development of jewelry among the Navajos underwent a number of phases. In the first phase, style and content were determined with little direct external influence; the market for the jewelry consisted entirely of Native Americans. This pure phase produced works that continue to serve as bench marks for Native American jewelry design in their simplicity and beauty. The elaborations of later phases, such as the addition of stones, incising, punching, and other decorative devices, continually yielded to the original, unelaborated style. At the same time that American art and craft of the last half of the 19th century pursued style with a European bias, new crafts arose in the American West that would profoundly influence the arts of the 20th century.

Contemporary jewelers work with a wide variety of stones, including traditional turquoise and coral, *left*. Stones and other jewelry-making materials and tools are available for puchase at big wholesale supply stores in Albuquerque and at trading posts near the reservation, where the jeweler can often sell the final product through the trader. Animal fetishes, *right*, come in a wide variety of sizes and materials.

Charles and Sharon Aberle have collected excellent examples of turquoise, coral, and shell necklaces. These early-style necklaces, *left and right,* are made of beads, painstakingly prepared and drilled. The rough and uncut surfaces of the turquoise indicate that it is from that first era of workmanship, when stones and silver tended to have a massive—even monumental—quality.

The concho belt derived from the silver hair plates worn by the Southern Plains Indians. Since these hair ornaments signified wealth, individuals wore as many as possible, hanging them down the back of the head. The longest chains had to be draped around the waist, which ultimately gave rise to the concho belt. The ornaments were round and massive, made of an alloy called German silver, which Navajos eventually adapted into conchos of their own, decorating them with incised designs and studding them with semiprecious stones. *At left,* Navajo women and girls display all of the essentials of Navajo women's dress at the fashion show held each year at Indian Market in Santa Fe. Besides concho belts, each woman wears a traditional velvet shirt and broomstick skirt. Millicent Rogers, a legendary figure in the 1940s in Taos, amassed a magnificent collection, *right,* now in the Millicent Rogers Museum.

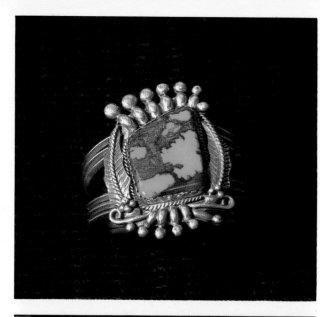

The massive turquoise ring, *bottom far left*, with a snake carved into the stone and the other bracelets and pins, *left*, as well as the beautiful double-cross coral necklace *right*, are all part of the extensive collection of Pueblo and Navajo jewelry formed by Millicent Rogers. An heiress of one of the partners in Standard Oil, Rogers had the taste, the means, and the energy to collect some of the best jewelry available during the late 1940s and early 1950s. Remarkably, she proceeded purely on an intuitive basis, collecting only what she liked.

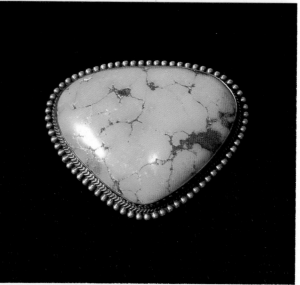

GAIL BIRD AND YAZZIE JOHNSON

As a youngster growing up in rural Winslow, Arizona, Yazzie Johnson knew that he would be an artist. In 1964 he set off to major in art at Utah State University, but ended up in Vietnam. Three years later he started pursuing his dream again and found himself in Berkeley, California, where he met Gail Bird. Like many young Native American artists, they decided to leave school and head for Santa Fe; both had friends in the community, and Gail had family at nearby Laguna Pueblo. There they began to piece together the necessary skills in silversmithing, along with a knowledge of and concern for traditional works. In 1972 they were back in school, this time at the University of Colorado, funded by scholarships and the sale of Yazzie's first work, a concho belt.

After a few years they realized that what they wanted to learn about jewelry would have to be discovered outside the classroom. Yazzie

Many of the tools that are used by Gail Bird and Yazzie Johnson, seen in their studio, *left,* have to be made by Yazzie, in order to meet their exacting criteria. *Right,* some of the handmade tools, stamps, skilled hands at work, and fine results in the Johnson studio, near Santa Fe.

began making his own tools, studying John Adair's groundbreaking *Navajo and Pueblo Silversmiths*, and studying old jewelry for construction techniques. By 1976 he had won first prizes in jewelry, sculpture, and painting at Santa Fe's Indian Market. In 1979 Gail and Yazzie began collaborating in the design and making of jewelry. Besides traditional materials, they began to innovate with unusual stones and mixed metals, such as silver and brass. A characteristic feature of their work is that each part, whether one of the medallions in the concho belt or an image in a bracelet, ultimately relates to the whole. With Gail's research methods, design skills, and passion for history and tradition and Yazzie's technical skills and understanding of traditional jewelry, they have formed an unusual collaboration that fuses their different backgrounds and sensibilities.

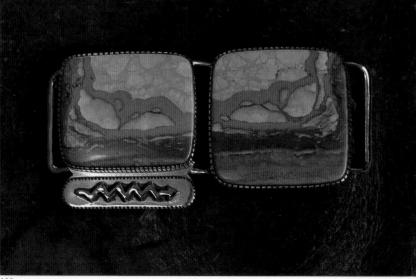

The imaginative use of nontraditional stones like jasper within a traditional context distinguishes the work of Gail Bird and Yazzie Johnson from that of other jewelers. Often they stamp the back of the piece with a motif that relates directly to the work on the front, a hidden pleasure for the owner.

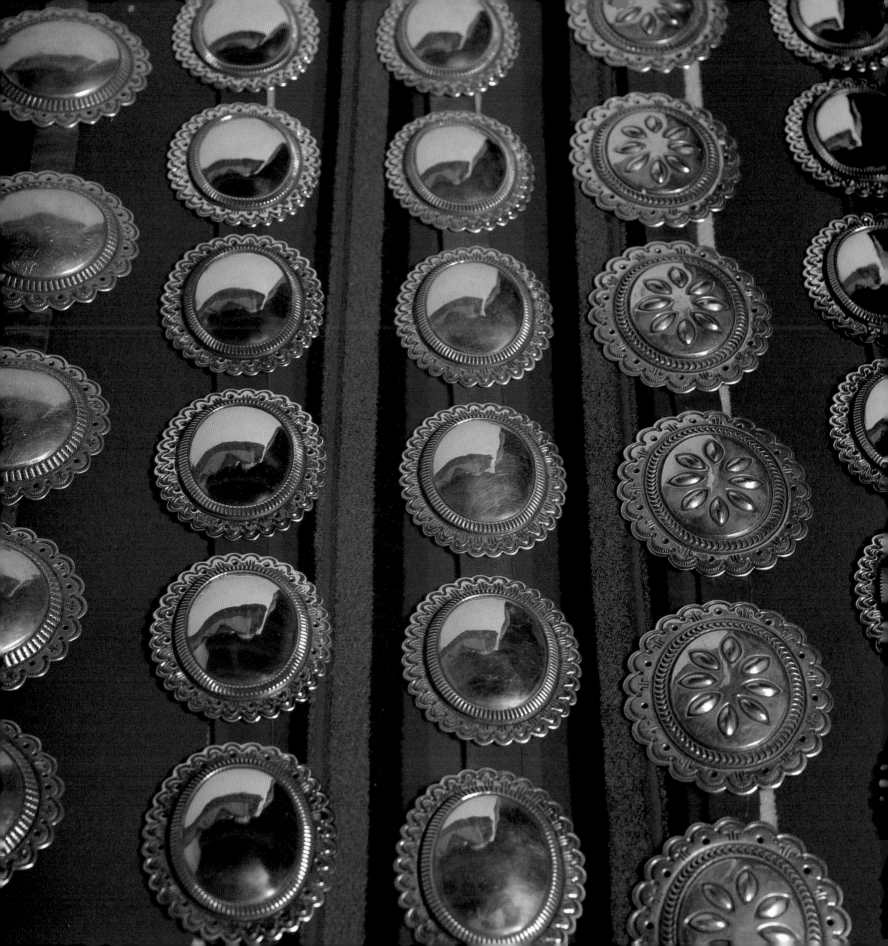

CIPPY CRAZY HORSE — COCHITI PUEBLO JEWELER

The pure and simple lines of classic Navajo and Pueblo silver jewelry serve as the unifying motif in the traditional work of Cippy Crazy Horse. Crazy Horse is a student of the past, researching the techniques of the early jewelers as well as archival photographs of their work. He has an added benefit to his pursuit of past purity, the opportunity to work within the legacy of his parents, both fine jewelers from Cochiti Pueblo, New Mexico.

The shining and plain surfaces of the conchos, *left,* and belts and bracelets, *above and above right,* reflect Cippy Crazy Horse's interest in the early phases of metalworking and jewelry in the region. Seated in his living room at Cochiti Pueblo, *right,* Cippy is surrounded by works by fellow artists he has collected.

TRADERS AND TOURISTS

Those who live in the West today still debate whether tourism is a curse or a blessing. The opening of the West to tourists with the railroad brought enormous changes that even today reverberate among the lives of the many who depend upon tourist dollars for their income. Although the relentless development that has all but erased the natural beauty of both coasts has not swept the desert Southwest (many Native American groups still live in relative isolation), the 20th century has brought most of Native America into the mainstream of American life. The promotional efforts of the railroad companies, and the hotels and tour

businesses established in their wake, brought the American Indian directly into contact with a restless consuming society. Almost overnight, arts and crafts that had important spiritual and functional aspects in Native society became curios and souvenirs.

The freewheeling entrepreneurs who guided clients through the West steered them to the sources for Indian goods, and coaxed Native artisans into adapting their traditions to meet tourist tastes. Colors, designs, size, function, decoration —all were dictated. The craftspeople themselves were even put on display, making Native America and Native Americans accessible—if romanticized—for the average tourist. What was lost, bastardized, distorted, and frivolized in this process truly cannot be reckoned.

After the traders came the historians and preservationists, and more tourists. The entire process of change, demise, and revival sometimes happened so quickly that the sequence of events was bewildering. The highway system, which followed upon the pathways developed by the railroad, became an even more efficient tourist route. Relentless numbers of billboads blocked views but hooked the visitor, who returned home laden with everything from cowboy hats to Navajo weavings. Plains Indian motifs had a special appeal: images of tipis and headdresses graced signs and sites many hundreds of miles from their proper origin. Lured by cactus candy, live buffalo, Hitler's touring car, tipi-shaped nightlights, and plastic embalmed scorpions, the diligent and enlightened traveler might unearth the real artifact. This remains true today: the most outrageous examples of tasteless Indian kitsch sometimes share the same display case with refined and legitimate crafts.

This trading post off Route 66 is a far cry from the original post on the reservation, where traders and Navajos met to trade, socialize, and catch up on reservation news. Old trading posts were centers of community life, and tourism played only a minor role. Today the emphasis is sometimes reversed.

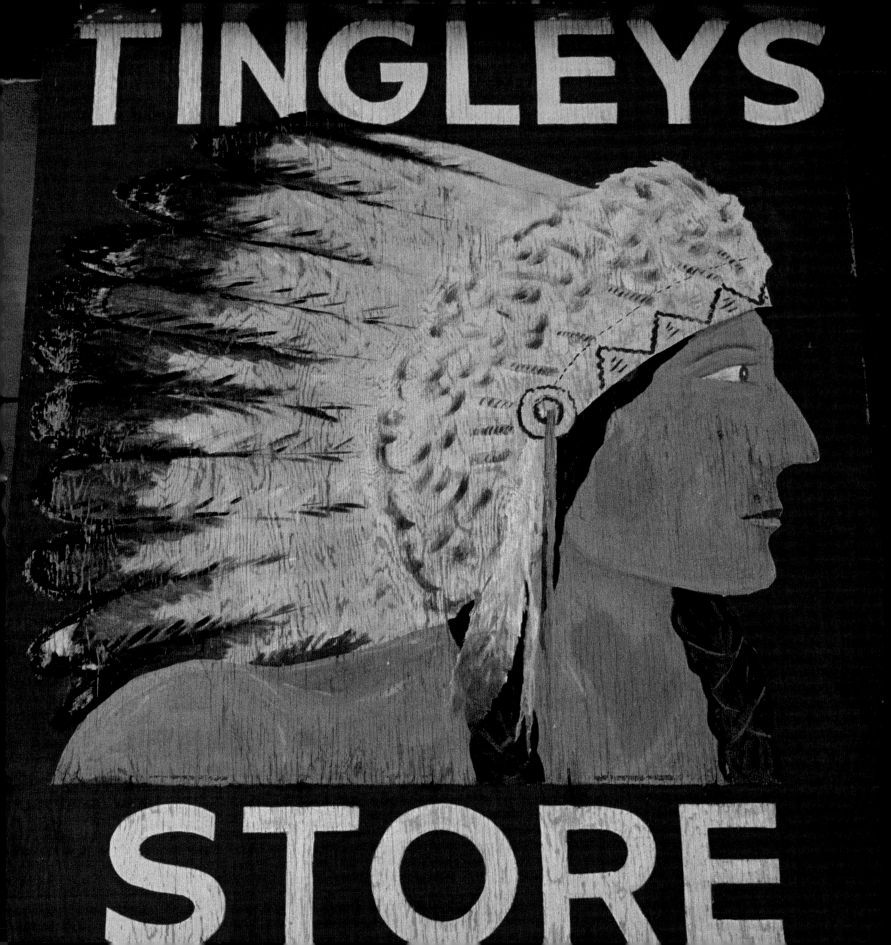

Once begun, the commercialization of Native America spread quickly. Now the slightly antique signs on these pages have become, however inaccurately, part of our romantic vision of the Wild West.

TRADI

TAKE A CHANCE

HANDCRAFTE PROD

WHOLESALE

Waterski NAVAJO School

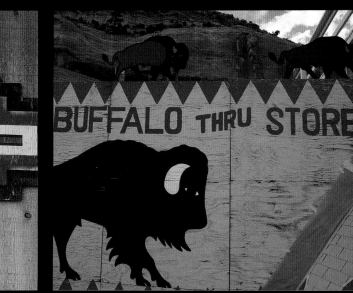

BUFFALO THRU STORE

A trading post like this one on the Navajo reservation in the 1940s, *left,* supplied everything from groceries to gas, but already the Navajo customer was being replaced by the tourist. The old trading posts, often located deep within the reservation beyond the reach of paved roads, continued to serve as real trading centers. *Above,* a gigantic concrete tipi serves as a three-dimensional billboard, dominating the landscape along the highway.

151

TRADING COMPANY

With the reservations came the trading post as a source of commercial products, a link with the cash economy, and an outlet for Native American goods.

The influence of the trading post in the Southwest remains undiminished today despite the ready availability of goods through discount stores, gas stations, convenience markets, and other commercial enterprises on the reservations. Today's trading posts still serve as the hub for the distribution of Native crafts to the buying public. In addition, the wealth of the Native community represented in jewelry is often stored in the vaults of the trading post waiting for display during special occasions. "Live pawn," as it is called, is the term for valuables left in the post's vault for a nominal fee. "Dead pawn," a much rarer commodity, is jewelry or other property left unclaimed beyond a specified period. Richardson's Trading Company in Gallup, New Mexico, at the southern edge of the Navajo reservation, still serves as a center for the trade and distribution of all the goods important to Navajo life.

Richardson's Trading Company in Gallup, New Mexico, has changed little in the last century. Navajos from all over the reservation still come to buy and sell, *left*, and the vaults are filled with "live pawn," *right*. The trading company still functions as a kind of safe deposit, where Navajos can store their valuables until they are needed.

The immense dignity and endurance of this Cheyenne elder, Honii-wotoma (Wolf Robe), is captured in this portrait of 1909 by DeLancey Gill. In his lifetime this warrior experienced the rigors of change as tribal lands and lifeways gave way to the demands of farmers, ranchers, and soldiers.

WAR
AND BEAUTY

With the coming of the horse to the New World, the destiny of the Native
Americans of the Great Plains changed forever. Their tipis have vanished with
their old ways, but the legends they inspired and the beautiful costumes
they made remain as testimony to a great people.

The formidable nomadic warrior peoples that dominated the Great Plains captured the world's imagination more than 100 years ago. Living symbols of the conflict between the past and the relentless future, the Cheyenne, Arapaho, Kiowa, Crow and Comanche, Sioux, and Apache inspired fear and respect among white settlers and peaceful nations alike. In an effort to establish access to hunting grounds and maintain their status as warriors, they conducted raids on other Native Americans, farming communities, and wagon trains, and in the last decades of the 19th century waged war against the U.S. Army.

Before the introduction of the horse by the Spanish between the 16th and 18th centuries, these nomadic groups followed on foot the migrations of the great herds of buffalo that populated the Plains. Dogs and women were the beasts of burden, transporting the household and the house—the famed tipi—from hunting camp to camp. Once mounted, the Plains Indian seemed to have met with a preordained destiny. All wealth and status became inextricably tied to the horse. In addition, territorial needs increased as a result of greater mobility. By the 19th century, the growing availability of guns and ammunition along with the beginnings of a westward expansion on the part of whites set the stage for an explosive series of confrontations among Native groups and later against the newest aggressors. The confrontational and sometimes unbelievably brutal ways of the Plains Indian were to be pitted against the demanding and sometimes unbelievably brutal ways of the white man. Un-

derscoring the physical conflict between the two groups was an even more profound dislocation caused by disease and by the virtual annihilation of the Indian's food source—the buffalo.

Among the soldier societies of the Plains Indians, the role of hunter was equally respected. Deer, antelope, rabbit, mountain sheep, and fowl were tracked with bow and arrow, but the buffalo was the primary food source. Every part of the animal was used. The preparation of the hides for clothing and shelter was women's work; its proper performance was regarded as essential and highly prestigious. Once scraped, softened, and fashioned into tipi liners, robes, and dresses, the hides were decorated with quills, beads, and other ornaments. The costumes, robes, and tipis of the Plains Indian were prized for beauty and durability.

As in many societies in which the warrior is supreme, hostility was paired with an unusual reverence for beauty and the mastery of poetry and music. The objects of war and the hunt—bow and quiver, spears, lances, shields, headdresses, fetishes, and later carbines—were accorded the greatest attention and respect. Songs and poems were addressed to horse and maiden alike. The difficulties of the hunter-warrior life were mirrored in the intensity of the life of the spirit. Vision quests, mortification of the flesh, and initiation rites often marked the world of the Plains Indian.

The large encampments of the Plains Indians, with their large, handsome tipis and the bustle of a vital and dignified people, is now gone. Annual gatherings held by various tribes are an opportunity for them to live together briefly as they once did.

On a clear day at the sacred site in Wyoming known as Medicine Wheel, *opposite,* you can see across plains that stretch beyond the imagination. Navajos, *top left,* though not riders of the plains, were proficient horsemen. White Horse, a Pawnee scout, 1868–1869, *above,* shows the merger of the American military costume with the Indian scout. The arrival of the horse in Native America facilitated the hunting of the American bison-buffalo, *left. Overleaf:* Assembled warriors of Big Foot's outfit against a backdrop at the Standing Rock Agency in North Dakota in the summer of 1890 are a dramatic sight.

"Big Bow" Kiowa Chief

THE WARRIOR

Warfare was continual among almost all Native American groups. The tactics and underlying reasons for aggression were far different, however, from the enormous conflicts that typified warfare among the so-called civilized nations. The warriors of Native America sought some of the usual rewards—spoils and status—but conflicts were acted out upon a vast, relatively unpopulated continent and consisted primarily of guerrillalike skirmishes among small numbers of combatants. Although groups defended hunting grounds and expanded territories through aggressive acts, there was no concept of sovereignty over people and borders such as fueled wars in Europe from the Middle Ages to World War II.

Warfare developed in Europe as a masculine conflict that consumed millions of lives over many years and involved complex military

The Kiowa and Apache scouts, chiefs, and warriors, *left and right,* became irresistible subjects for the frontier photographer. Their traditional dress of leather and ornament was mixed with U.S. military equipment and hardware in ingenious combinations. Despite the false shrubbery and painted backdrops of the studio, these Native American men project toughness, self-assurance, and character.

tactics and concepts of honor and discipline according to a military code. Native American conflicts by contrast involved few fighters, were usually quickly resolved, and were guided more by the instinct for self-preservation. Native American fighters were instrumental in the founding of our country since their tactics as well as some of the warriors themselves—such as the Iroquois—were used with great effectiveness by both the French and the British. Ultimately, however, the short-term advantages of guerrilla warfare could not withstand the highly organized, well-supported, technically superior, disciplined, and self-sustaining institutions that came to invade the Native American land-

The development of the bow and arrow came relatively late to the New World, but with it came great advantages to the hunter.

scape, primarily in the form of the U.S. Army.

Among Native Americans, conflict was traditionally between communities and involved some form of long-cultivated enemy relationship. Often skirmishes were more ritualized than totally devastating, emphasizing the individual's role and needs in achieving manhood or reaching a quota of "coup." Loyalty and discipline certainly played a part in the effective arsenal of the Native warrior, but not at the cost of self-determination. If the spirit world seemed to be particularly unpropitious on a certain day, a warrior did not go to war—a hanging offense in Western culture. Given this background, Native Americans had no hope of defeating the U.S. Government's goals of subduing Indian populations and controlling territory.

Tomahawks, *above,* were used in hand-to-hand combat. At Western artist Harvey W. Johnson's studio, *left and right,* are the many accoutrements of the plainsmen and the Plains Indian. Objects of war and the hunt were often ornately decorated to show the value and respect the warrior had for his weapons.

The Chippewa warrior wears a three-feathered version that probably indicated his rank and successes

F ar more than mere decoration, feathers were important elements of ceremonial dress and ritual, symbols of power and prestige throughout Native America. The use of feathers was often proscribed or restricted to those who performed specific feats of valor. In addition to shooting birds on the wing, some groups even raised or kept birds tethered, particularly birds of prey, so that feathers would be available when needed for specific ceremonies.

Feathers are found dangling from pipes, as parts of sacred bundles, on women's and men's dress alike, on fans, woven into textiles and baskets, and in a wide variety of ceremonial contexts. Feather heraldry varied greatly among Plains Indians as well as within the important male societies. The elaborate "war bonnet" associated with Plains groups had its origins in the Eastern Woodlands and traveled westward to the grasslands.

The ceremonial powwow dancer seen at the Red Earth Festival in Oklahoma City, *above far right*, features an elaborate and creative use of feathers. The feather fans like those *above right and right* were used during peyote ceremonies of the Native American Church.

The most common and useful of the weapons of the early arsenal was the spear, widely used in the arduous task of hunting both small and large game. As young men, Native American hunters and warriors learned these skills not only through daily practice, but also through competitive games that tested accuracy, endurance, and aggressiveness. Today's youth, *right,* learn the history of their group and practice the tradition in ceremonies and other gatherings.

When going into battle the Plains Indian always dressed for the occasion. His choice of garments and decoration came not as much from a need for physical armor as from a necessity for spiritual protection. Except for the shield, which was quite effective, few of the costume parts could be expected to protect the wearer from bodily harm. The warrior did bring to the battle all the supernatural help he could muster, however, and to this end the garments and the warrior were carefully decorated. The elaborate beading of the contemporary powwow costume of this young man is an extension of his warrior ancestor's attention to self-preservation through the use of symbol and talismans.

The powwow, as it is practiced today, draws together diverse elements of the Native American community. At the heart of the powwow is the underlying unity of the Native American experience, which transcends the many differences between traditional groups. The gathering can be a simple family reunion or a spectacle on a grand scale involving thousands of participants. Large powwows, such as the one at the Red Earth Festival in Oklahoma in June, *left and right,* occur throughout the country and involve competitive costume, music, and dance events. Straight Dance, War Dance, Traditional Dance, and Grass Dance are common programs for men and boys, each awarding cash prizes to the winners. To the young and athletic, the summer powwow circuit may be a means of earning school money for the fall. For most, it is the opportunity to renew ties and friendships and to pass on the traditions of dance and music.

HORSES

Horses, first brought to the continent by the Spanish in the 16th century, sparked a revolution in Native American life by the early years of the 18th century. The enormous advantages afforded by the horse transformed the once grueling and demanding life of the nomadic hunter. More efficient hunting created food surpluses, which in turn increased populations. Larger territories could be defended with more effective warfare. Able to cover enormous distances, fight from his running mount, and inspire fear in almost any opponent, the mystic warrior had a brief romantic history on the Great Plains.

Deified, sought after, prized, decorated, and even serenaded, the horse became the central feature of Plains culture. Horse raids between tribes and upon Spanish and Anglo-American settlements were commonplace. Comanches in particular acquired thousands of horses, along with a reputation for unparalleled fierceness as warriors. The great value placed on the horse is demonstrated by the lavish adornment of saddles, bags, and other trappings.

At Crow Fair in Montana, young and old show off their finery from horseback as they parade among friends and onlookers.

A Crow woman's horse, *left*, waits patiently for its rider. The horse's elaborate beaded trappings require the same degree of attention, creativity, and care as the costume of the rider.

The beaded pendant, *above*, and pouches, *left and below*, from the Thomas Gilcrease Museum in Tulsa, Oklahoma, show the artisans' fascination with the horse.

Soft hide gloves, *below*, also from the Gilcrease Museum, were likely made for the non-Indian market.

The interrelationship of beaded decoration, fringed leather, ribbons, hairdressing, and other decoration adds up to a stunning overall appearance. Early garments, like those of the Ute woman, *above*, were quite weighty and would never have been used as everyday apparel but only for important or festive occasions.

BEAUTY AND THE BEAD

The simple decorative device of the bead can be used to trace much of the history of America. Both in pre- and postcontact periods beads were an important trading commodity. Before the arrival of Europeans, shells were traded thousands of miles inland and were carved, ground, and formed into exquisite ornaments. Columbus remarked on the enthusiasm with which beads were accepted during his first contacts with Native Americans, and the importance of beads as trade goods remained undiminished for hundreds of years. As the importance of glass beads grew, shells, stone beads, quills, feathers, and embroidery gradually disappeared as decorative devices. Native Americans strung beads into necklaces and used them as currency—"wampum"—and appliquéd them upon garments. In the area of decorating leather finery, the humble glass bead made the greatest impact.

Red Feather

Spanning 100 years in the life of their tribe, the Sioux women, *above and right,* show off their traditional ceremonial dress.

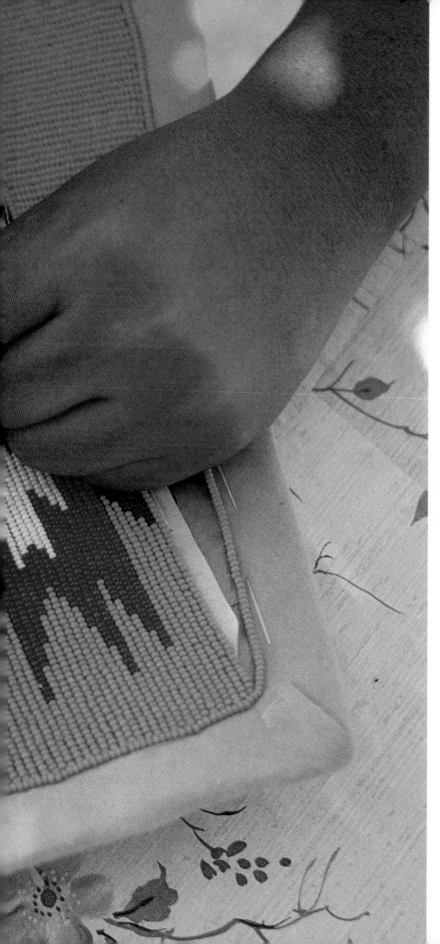

A beadworker labors on a pair of beaded cuffs while attending the annual gathering at Crow Fair in Montana, *left.* Such costume parts are added gradually to the finery of the owner or are received as important gifts among family members and friends as well as being passed from generation to generation.

The Sioux women White Rose, *above,* and Tells Me, *above right,* display their finery. Shells and elk's teeth on the women's garments reflect the status that these older women achieved in their lifetimes.

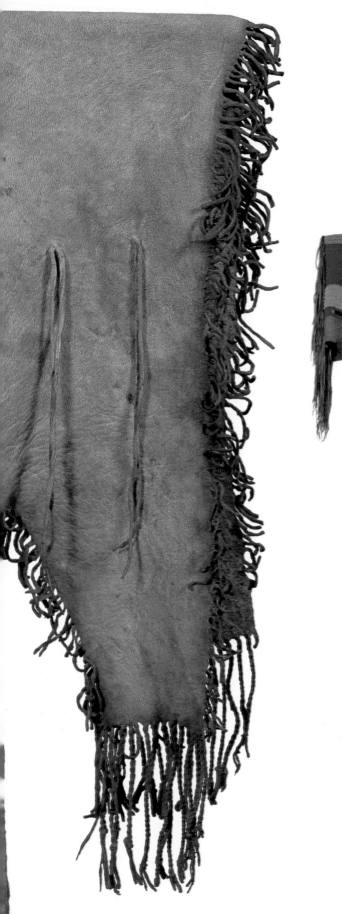

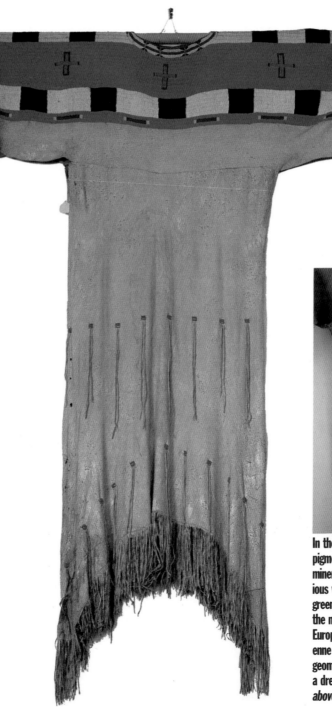

In the Comanche child's painted dress, *far left*, pigments for the paints were obtained from mineral-rich clays, ground and mixed with various vehicles for application to leather. Blues, greens, and especially true reds were some of the more difficult pigments to obtain prior to European contact. A late-19th-century Cheyenne dress, *left*, is decorated completely with geometric designs; beadwork horses decorate a dress in the collection of Nedra Matteucci, *above*.

Carefully strung bone makes handsome ornaments, such as breastplates, *above and right,* which can be worn by men or women and are often combined with beads. At powwows and other gatherings Native Americans have an opportunity to come together to admire costumes accumulated over a lifetime, carefully augmented with gifts from friends and relatives.

Shells were trade goods in both prehistoric and historic times and were considered to be very valuable commodities; the use of shells and bone for costumes was common throughout Native America. The collar of the Blackfoot woman, *left,* made entirely of sewn-on dentalium shells, shows the extent to which shells could enhance a garment. The embroidery, *above,* is a simpler form of ornament that also requires excellent sewing skills.

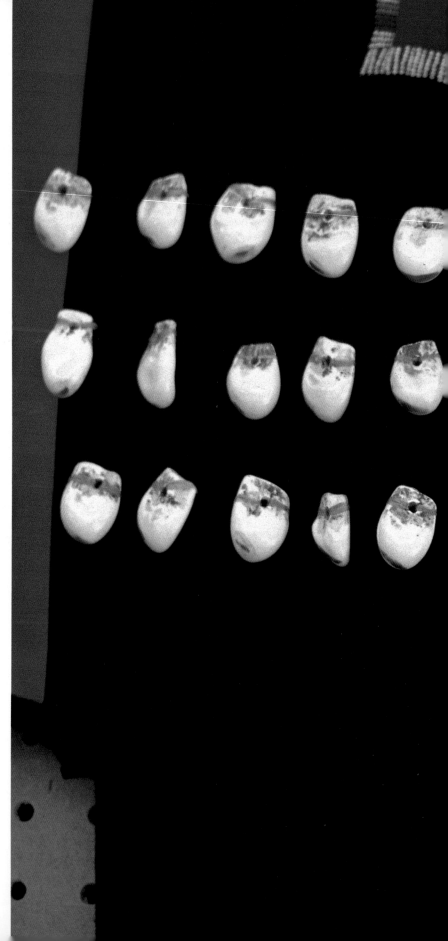

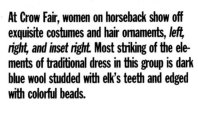

At Crow Fair, women on horseback show off exquisite costumes and hair ornaments, *left, right, and inset right.* Most striking of the elements of traditional dress in this group is dark blue wool studded with elk's teeth and edged with colorful beads.

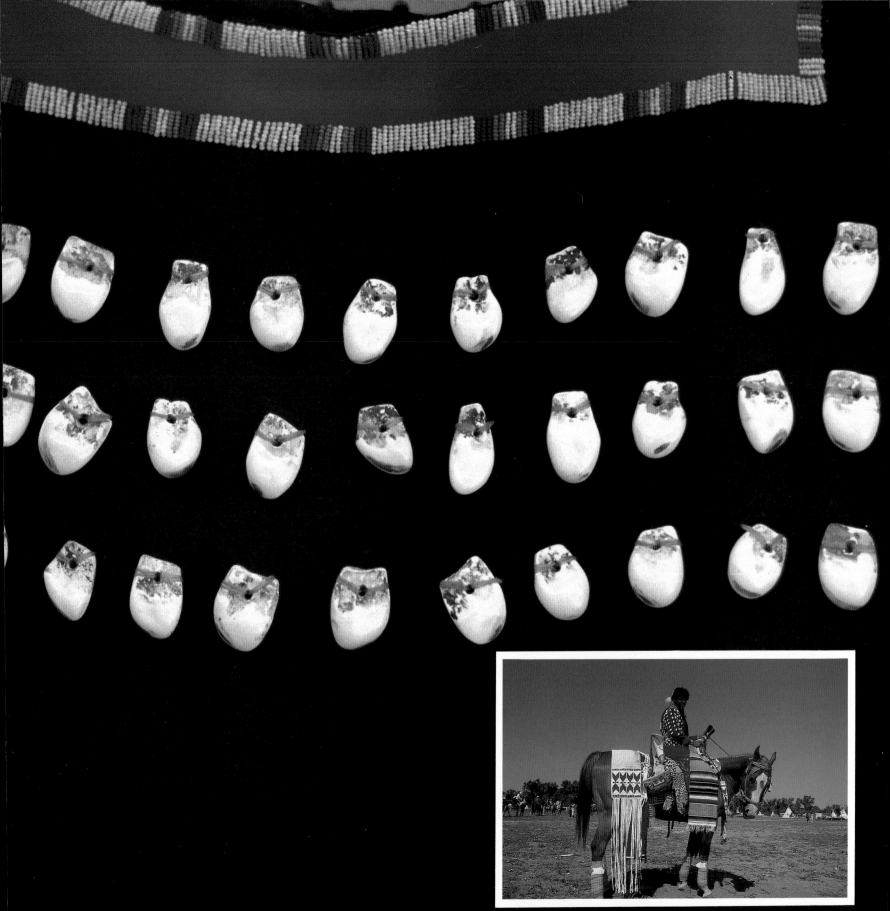

On these two pages, Patricia McClure of Arlee, Montana, wears jewelry made for her by her mother, Rachael Arlee Bowers. Bead embroidery did not develop in the northern Plains until after 1840, and it was not until later in the century that small glass beads became available. Traditionally Plains designs were rich in geometric shapes—triangles, hourglass shapes, crosses, rectangles, diamonds, and squares. Today these designs ornament a host of objects, including necklaces, earrings, barrettes, bracelets, belts, and bolo ties. Beads may be woven on a bead loom, hand-strung, or stitched.

Braiding and decorating hair is common among Plains women. Before the introduction of the comb, Native Americans fashioned ingenious grooming devices—a porcupine tail mounted on a stick, stiff grass bound like a small broom, and even the rough side of a buffalo tongue. Often hair was parted in the middle and the part painted red. Some groups let their hair hang long; others tied the braids together.

A common locker, *left,* makes an effective display case for very rare dresses from the Plains. Fully beaded dresses weigh up to twenty pounds. On the top shelf are a collection of beaded moccasins and a beaded doctor's bag. An array of small beaded pouches from the Thomas Gilcrease Museum, Tulsa, Oklahoma, *right,* includes carrying pouches and, *at bottom center,* a mirror and "kit" used to carry pigments to make up a warrior.

AGNES KENMILLE AT FLATHEAD LAKE

Agnes Kenmille seems to lead a life that is totally steeped in tradition while completely in tune with the spirit of the times. She is thoroughly independent and self-sufficient, and possesses a rare range of knowledge about the proper preparation of skins and the beading of the ceremonial dress, moccasins, and crown.

A small shed behind her compact wooden house on the shores of Flathead Lake in Montana serves as Kenmille's workshop. There she takes the fresh deerskins, scrapes them carefully to remove the flesh and hair, and reworks the surface to create a soft, supple skin.

The intricacies of the floral beadwork on the shoulders of the dress made and decorated by Agnes Kenmille of Flathead Lake, Montana, are seen clearly in the detail, *left*. Agnes's crown and moccasins, *above right and right*, have the same red rose motif. She shows her renowned skills at leatherwork, *above*, scraping a hide with a homemade tool.

CRADLED IN BEAUTY

Within a few weeks of birth, the Native American infant could often be found carefully strapped into a cradleboard—its viewing platform of its new world for the coming year. Among Pueblo groups the cradleboard was primarily a device for holding the baby while it was fed, cared for, and rocked to sleep. Among Plains Indians the cradleboard served more as a means of transportation; it was supported on

The Apache mothers and babies on cradleboards were photographed in the studio of Ben Wittick in the 1880s, *left and above.* Among cradleboards brought together by the Oklahoma obstetrician Dr. Harry Deupree are examples from Hopi, Hupa, Salish, Santo Domingo, and Navajo, as well as a handsome and rare wooden Mohawk cradle, *right.*

the mother's back by a strap across her forehead, slung upon a saddle, or placed between the two trailing poles of a primitive vehicle called a travois. The elaborate beaded decoration of the cradleboard was often the work of a close female relative, and is a clear indication of the regard with which a new life was greeted within the family and community.

Among the earliest collectors of cradleboards was Dr. Harry Deupree. In 1934, while he was still in medical school, Deupree used what little money he had to purchase his first cradleboard, a handsome beaded Cheyenne example. With the greatest of good luck he met up with Minnie Blackbear, who recognized it as one that she had made.

As an obstetrician in Oklahoma, Dr. Deupree had many Native American patients, since he was fascinated by their art and lives and proud of his wife's Choctaw-Chickasaw heritage. During a lifetime of delivering Native Americans into the world and attending their mothers, Deupree amassed one of the most impressive private collections, which he gave to the Center of the American Indian in Oklahoma City.

The archival photograph, *top right,* of Umatilla twin girls Tox-e-lox and A-lom-pum was taken by Lee Moorehouse, ca. 1898. It is one of a pair of photographs; the second shows the babies wailing simultaneously. The handsome beaded buckskin cradleboard, *above,* was made for a Ute baby born about 1880. One wall of the study of Dr. Harry Deupree, *right,* shows a number of Plains Indian cradleboards, as well as peyote fans, beaded moccasins, and doll cradleboards. Future Native American mothers were often given miniature cradleboards and dolls as playthings.

MOCCASINS

Many different types of moccasins were made throughout Native America: hard-soled and soft-soled, high-top and low-cut. They were made from everything from buffalo hide to salmon skin, and their decoration was even more varied. Some moccasins were suited to the rough, prickly terrain of the Southwest; others provided extra warmth and protection against Arctic environments; still others served as the canvas upon which a proficient Plains beadworker might display her skills.

Among Plains Indians, distinctive designs and techniques came into being during the period of growth and conflict of the latter half of the 19th century. The construction of the moccasin, the technique of applying the decoration, and the patterns and designs are clues to the tribal affiliation of the maker.

Above left, a pair of Sioux men's moccasins, decorated with porcupine quills, were collected at the Pine Ridge Reservation in South Dakota near Wounded Knee. *Left,* the beautiful pair of painted Pueblo Indian moccasins was intended for special or ceremonial usage, not for everyday wear.

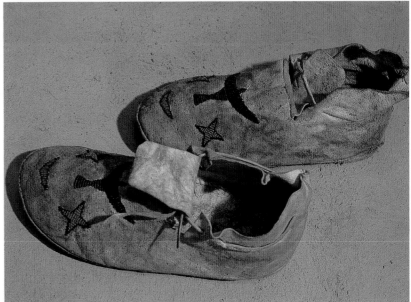

During the late 19th century and with the spread of beadwork throughout the Plains, regional variations in designs and techniques began to appear. Geometric designs as well as representations of animals or other objects had meaning for both the wearer and the maker—but sometimes different meanings—and the use of color symbolized different things, depending on the location.

Fringed and decorated leggings like these brought warmth and protection to their Plains Indian owner.

The pantheon of animal deities was incorporated into art and dance as in this headpiece surmounted by a loon. Edward S. Curtis, the most famous photographer of American Indians, took this portrait of a Northwest Coast elder and also filmed dance sequences of the region's tribes.

TOTEM

From past to present, the Northwest Coast has been a Native American
region rich in myth and drama. Totem poles once edged
great villages; today they inspire us with the power of the spirit world
and the unsurpassed skills of their carvers.

The Indians of the Northwest Coast have a long history of settlement in the coastal environment once connected to the Asian continent. Their refined arts and large populations brought to the history of Native America one of its most important chapters. Despite the many different language groups and successive waves of migration into the region, they shared a maritime culture in which hunting and fishing were paramount and agriculture was nonexistent. The focus of their culture, both as a source of food and a feature of ritual, was the salmon.

The Northwest Coast people observed the salmon's seasonal movements between fresh and salt water. Along with the scrutiny of the behavior of other important animal species such as the seal and bear, these observations served as the basis for much of the ritual life of the Northwest Coast. Here, where an abundance of natural resources supported a large and concentrated population, matters of kinship and clan took on significance. The enactment of the important kinship as well as other ritual renewals took place within an all-important institution—the potlatch.

Potlatch was and still remains today a complex institution that establishes economic stability, reaffirms status and kinship ties, and imparts an overall sense of emotional well-being and continuity for the people. To potlatch is to give. In giving, the one who potlatches receives confirmation of status and certain kinship rights. Among these rights are included significant songs and dances as well as the use of certain symbols or crests. The complexity of the potlatch cannot be minimized nor can it be directly related to Western European institutions.

At the potlatch and throughout the long winter season, the people of the Northwest brought forth their entire pantheon of deities in intense, theatrical dances and reenactments. The mythological world was brought to life and gave substance and meaning to existence. Dance, song, costumes, and masks accompanied the rituals.

The making and raising of a totem pole was another important event, an acknowledgment of the new rights conferred by the potlatch as well as a gesture of honor to a forebear; the totem pole contains all of the totems of the ancestor. Even the most utilitarian of objects within Northwest Coast societies bears careful decoration, but these monumental tiers of figures and faces are their most inspiring works. Here was a formalized, highly structured method of pictorial representation that at first defied the comprehension of even the most sophisticated of outside observers. The flattened geometry contains a codified and demanding means of depiction that is every bit as complex as the iconography of Western art.

The totem poles that lined the housefronts, guarded the cemeteries, and stood as sentries at the edges of the villages represent a pinnacle of achievement among Northwest Coast artisans.

Today the work of the mask and totem pole maker is undergoing a renaissance. Even though potlatches were once suppressed and great collections of ceremonial objects were dispersed, the identity of the people through their art was gradually reasserted through the work of the Northwest Coast wood-carver and the reassertion of the potlatch in community life.

At the farthest reach of the continental United States are the coastal waters of the Makah people at Neah Bay on the Olympic Peninsula in Washington, *opposite and top*. They have fished and hunted along this coast for over 500 years and continue to do so today. *Above*, Haida fisherfolk set out to sea from their village of Kasaan. Far to the north in Port Clarence, Alaska, Eskimos prepare ivory and mukluks, ca. 1900, *below left*.

FACES OF THE PAST

Along the narrow strip of inhabitable land between sea and mountains that extends from Alaska to northern California lived the extraordinary people of the Northwest Coast. Although strong in numbers due to the amazing abundance of the fauna of sea and land, like other Native peoples of North America they were never organized as a greater unit. The very distinct groups of this area have come to be recognized by language as follows: Tlingit, Haida, Tsimshian, Northern and Southern Kwakiutl, Bella Coola, West Coast, and Coast Salish. Other groups, most notably Inuit populations to the north, lived within a much more demanding ecosystem and may have been among the last Native groups to enter North America. In any case, the archeological record indicates man's presence in this area at some of the oldest sites at 8,500 years ago.

The variety, beauty, detail, and intensity of Northeast Coast costumes can be seen in these late 19th- and early 20th-century portraits of different peoples along the coast, *left from top left clockwise:* two Haida artists, ca. 1895; a gathering of chiefs from the Kwakiutl nation, 1914; a couple in ceremonial costume, 1913; a woman with woven red cedar garment and hat adorned with shells. *Right,* Qa'Hila-Koprino looks directly into the camera of Edward S. Curtis in 1914. In addition to the traditional garment of woven cedar bark the Northwest Coast native wears an ornament in his nose.

POTLATCH
AT
ALERT BAY

For raw drama, theatricality, and beauty, few events are more powerful than the potlatch. Sometimes years in the making, the potlatch involves all of the kin of the giver and hundreds of others who gather to confirm his or her rank and prestige. All celebrants bring out their finest ceremonial regalia: rattles, masks, robes, drums, and frontlets. Important relationships are affirmed by inviting relatives to join in the dance, which enacts mythic events between the world of the supernatural—often in the form of animals—and man. Dancers, who diligently perfect their mimickry of the animals they portray, become bees, birds, bears, and other creatures that make up the Northwest Coast pantheon.

Drama is intensified by the flickering, smoky light from the central bonfire in the large hall. In this atmosphere the supernatural beings of the Northwest Coast return to circle the fire and bring the spirit world to life.

This potlatch, given by the Hunt family in 1988 in Alert Bay, British Columbia, comprised two days of food, dance, and song, culminating in a final gift-giving ceremony. Dancers, *left and right,* assume the characteristics of the animals they represent—bird, bee, or whale—as they circle the fire in the center of the Big House.

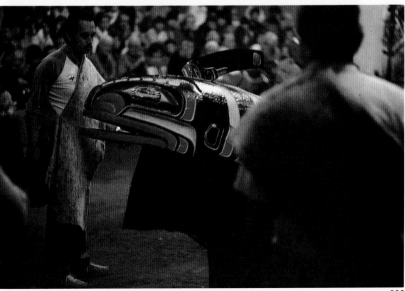

RETURN TO ALERT BAY

Whether from missionaries or from government officials, all of the Northwest Coast people saw their traditional ways under attack in the 19th century. The Southern Kwakiutl put up the greatest resistance. By 1884 Canada had drafted laws to ban potlatch ceremonies, but the Southern Kwakiutl continued to create their ritual paraphernalia and ceremonies. Then in 1921 disaster struck at Alert Bay: government agents seized all the potlatch ritual artifacts and costumes and arrested the community leaders who had worked to maintain tribal traditions. The potlatch went underground, but the memory of the tragic event and the treasures that had been lost remained. By 1980 part of the stolen property finally returned to Alert Bay, British Columbia, where it is now housed in a special museum.

Some of the government-confiscated potlatch returned to the people has been put on permanent display at the U'Mista Cultural Center in Alert Bay. These masks, *left and right,* are not merely decorative objects or even just art treasures; they are sacred totems of the heritage of Alert Bay.

ART THOMPSON WEST COAST CARVER

Art Thompson's affiliation is with the people of the West Coast of Vancouver Island in British Columbia. Because vigorous government intervention in the early 20th century all but obliterated the traditions of the region, the new generation of wood-carvers had to rediscover the forms and methods of their ancestral art. Working with archival data, studying the objects of the past, and experimenting with tools and materials, contemporary carvers have revived the knowledge that historically they would have acquired through years of apprenticeship with a close male relative. Thompson's work spans a range of media and techniques—totem poles, masks, drums, and prints. All incorporate the spirit and subjects of West Coast art.

The West Coast artist Art Thompson, *above*, has many works in progress at the same time, from full-size totem poles to subtle, smaller-scale masks, such as the human mask, *left*.

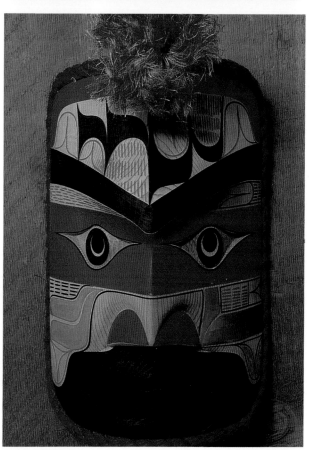

Each of the human and portrait masks by Art Thompson, *left and above center*, possesses strong graphic qualities that reflect the traditional compositions and subjects of Northwest Coast art. Thompson also prepares and paints drums with similar motifs, *top and bottom*.

TO THE REDWOOD FORESTS

The Northwest Coast offers all of the riches of the natural world. Air warmed by the Japanese Current drops its wealth of moisture when it reaches the high coastal range. From this rainfall come the vast redwood forests as well as abundant wildlife. The sea also gave a bounty to the people and animals of the land. The riches of this unique environment were reflected in the material culture of the coastal people of the Northwest. Despite the various groups their shared life-style gave to all a shared emphasis—upon personal property and prestige. Nowhere in the indigenous world of North America was greater focus placed upon the ownership of rights. The rights that

In the 1920s at Alert Bay, poles lined the bay and guarded the cemeteries, *below and bottom.* Representing the highest era of achievement among Northwest Coast artisans, these massive cedar posts were carved with myriad images of the clan deities. *At right,* a massive array of totem poles lines the front of the Haida village of Skidegate.

a chief might claim for himself and his kin included an enormous range of both the tangible and the ephemeral. From berry patches to individual songs and dances were "things" which might be claimed. Ritual and ceremony were in support of claimed rights. The visual arts developed in direct response to the need for assuring lineage and the rights of the individual. Clan and heraldry were of paramount importance; without the ability to claim and secure one's rights the social fabric would be destroyed. One result of this emphasis was the creation of many material goods; the skilled wood-carver, the creator of songs, the best dancers or fishermen were persons of great value since they could add materially to the wealth of a leader. Leadership was determined by heredity and lineage so that any leader was engaged in a constant process of maintaining and claiming his ancestry.

Objects became part of this emphasis upon lineage. A fine ceremonial bowl would be passed from generation to generation, its value increasing with age since it represented a connection with an ancestor of the past. The most important object that proclaimed the lineage and ownership of rights came in the form of the totem pole.

The transient nature of organic material in the wet coastal regions has made it difficult to trace the development of the totem pole among the people of the Northwest Coast. It is believed that the pole was a natural extension of the enormous house posts of both domestic and ceremonial structures. Enormous by any standard, they were erected to serve as dwellings for large, extended families. Of posts and planks, the

Every totem pole is a unique compilation of carvings of subjects from the mythology of the owner's tribe and family. Most characters are representations of animals, birds, and humans, which in turn signify stories and traditions meaningful to the owner, as in the examples *above*. The imposing Cedar Bear, *left*, was carved by Bill Reid in 1966. It is now at the University of British Columbia Museum of Anthropology, Vancouver. Bill Reid is probably the best known of the Northwest Coast artists. The son of a Haida mother and an Anglo father, he has become a bridge between traditional culture and mainstream 20th-century art. A versatile sculptor in gold, bronze, and cedar, his exquisite jewelry and monumental totem poles have led to his designation as one of Canada's National Living Treasures.

The details of two totem poles carved by Bill Holms of Seattle, *left and right*, show the intensity that can be achieved in this art form. Holms, an anthropologist and artist, learned by doing. For years he studied these monumental works by copying them, eventually publishing his understanding of their function and meaning in his *Northwest Coast Indian Art: An Analysis of Form.* In addition to his contribution as a scholar, he also became, through this study technique, a master carver of the Northwest Coast.

redwood structures had within large central posts that served as a surface upon which to carve aspects of family ancestry. Matters of clan and kinship often took animal form in conformance with myth and creation. Claims of ancestry to various animals were carefully proscribed and jealously guarded. The sheer weight of protocol in ceremonial behavior was immense. Carved posts that emphasized and proclaimed ancestry were placed not only within the structure but also on the exterior and eventually became freestanding elements used not only to proclaim village and family prerogatives but also as cemetery art.

As wealth increased in the coastal villages so did the number of poles, so that during the 19th century the village fronts had the appearance of a forest of totem poles. With the emphasis upon material property and heraldry came a concomitant focus upon size. The potlatch put high merit upon the amount of goods, the largess of the gifts; bowls and tables were made to "groan" with food and the masks of the dancers were outsized. Largest of all were the grand poles which stood outside the Great Houses. Ceremony, myth, and the material world they sought to propitiate—all were made to be larger than life.

This man figure, *right*, appears on a totem pole in Thunderbird Park, part of the Victoria Provincial Museum complex in Victoria, British Columbia. Created in 1940, the park was established as a showcase for the wood-carver's art, both early, protected examples of totem poles and other carvings and monumental sculpture by contemporary carvers.

Common totem pole representations are the thunderbird, bear, raven, wolf, whale, frog, and beaver. Since mythology usually endowed these creatures with human characteristics, the carvings often have a combination of human and animal features. Human figures might also be represented. On this page are a singing man with an extended arm topped by a thunderbird, *right*; a man and beast combination, *above far right*; and a very humanoid beaver, *far right*.

Drums, as adjuncts to the dance and other ceremonies, have always played an important role in Northwest Coast cultures, and artists still create them today. The images on each drum refer to specific legends that are important to the maker. The drums on these pages are, *left, clockwise from top far left,* Greg Colfax's Mother Bear and Cub, Colfax's Raven Eating Salmon Eggs, Spencer McCarty's Creation Story Drum, Colfax's Raven, and Colfax's Whale; and *right,* a Welcome Drum by Spencer McCarty.

"Button blankets" like this one, made and worn by Eileen David, *below,* were traditionally dark blue wool with red flannel appliqué and pearl buttons. Unique to the Northwest Coast, they proclaim hereditary rights, obligations, and powers at a more personal level than the totem poles. The blanket and hat worn by Joe Kennelka, chief of the Dasheton family, Tlingit, in a photo by George Emmons, 1888, *right,* features the clan symbol, a beaver.

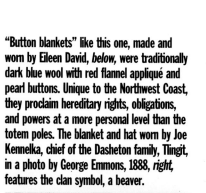

Beautiful woven and painted hats were worn on ceremonial occasions. A classic photograph by Edward S. Curtis, taken in 1914, *left,* illustrates their delicacy of weave and artistry of design. The subject is Nakoaktok, a chief's daughter. *Above,* Dorothy Grant models a hat she wove in the traditional manner, with a dress inspired by the red-and-blue cut and appliquéd button robes.

ETERNAL RETURN

One of the threads that runs through the life of Native America is the artful embellishment of the everyday, objects as well as activities. This transformation of the prosaic into the beautiful has as one of its major sources the relationship between the young and old, the past and present, and the child and elder. The sense of continuity and the slow and purposeful unfolding of life from its fragile beginnings to its inevitable end allow each human act and stage in the journey to have a significance that can be read and imagined in everyday objects. In each newborn, Native Americans recognize the ongoing survival of the people and in each elder, reverence for the past.

Regardless of the culture—Mohawk, Flathead, Pueblo, or Sioux—the relationship between child and adult is marked by the respect that the young accord  the old and by the affection and concern of the old for the young. A child brought into this world may be greeted by objects that display its great importance to its family and tribe. In the complex beadwork of the cradleboard, the simple elegance of a cornhusk doll, or the humor of a clay figure are the elements of a long tradition. As he or she grows and learns to make such things as a cornhusk doll or pottery figure, the Native American child begins to appreciate the skill, time, and care that went into the objects of childhood, perhaps undertaking an apprenticeship of his or her own. The children of Native America have a unique opportunity to re-create the experiences of their past and to create works of art that have served for centuries as a means of communication and of binding the individual to the group. In the dances and songs, in the stories and myths, lie the legends and knowledge of the past. In the works of art lie the archives of the people. Art becomes a dialogue through which the old and the young might perpetuate the life of their tribe.

Continuity of tradition may be taken for granted by many Americans, but not by those whose culture has been threatened for hundreds of years. Almost since the arrival of the first European settlers, the recorded history of Native America has been one of loss—loss of land, culture, and people. The romanticized image of the vanishing American Indian pervades our visual and literary arts from Longfellow's "Hiawatha" to TV westerns. Yet, remarkably, despite their suffering, Native Americans have maintained a cultural identity that has continued to develop, enriching the lives of all Americans with objects of unparalleled beauty and deeply spiritual oral traditions. For the early settlers of the 17th to 19th centuries, America's resources seemed endless. Now, as it becomes clear that as a nation we have squandered much of the original bounty of the continent, we have begun to appreciate the precious and fragile relationship between man and nature. The lessons to be learned from Native Americans, who knew the land first and respect nature's gifts, will be a legacy to be shared by all in the centuries to come. Equally important is the preservation of the artifacts of the past and the ongoing vigor of the contemporary crafts movement—a tangible source of inspiration for Native Americans and their many non-Indian admirers.

The tradition of Native American life, then and now, is one faithfully passed on from the elders to the youth through the cycle of generations. The faces on these pages reflect 100 years of Pueblo history —a story of continuity, creativity, and caring.

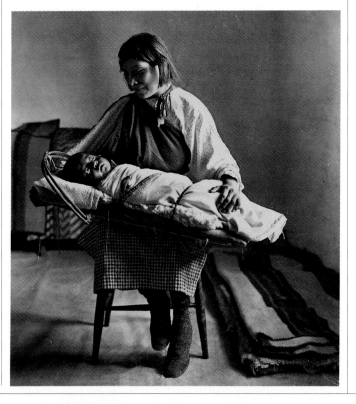

THE ELDERS

Yes, my children, I am the storage box of your thoughts, for I remember all the old tales, and in my young days I saw things which you young people never heard of. It is good that there is one old man who can show you all these things.

—Tugwamalis, speaker for the Gusgimukw, Fort Rupert, British Columbia, 1895

The elders of Native America have a clear vision of themselves as mentors. It is their duty and their joy to pass on the knowledge of the past as given to them by *their* elders. Around countless kitchen tables, in makeshift workshops, at community houses or school buildings, in front of television sets, at powwows and tribal ceremonies, older tribal members work constantly and consistently at the task of handing on their knowledge.

The older generation of today's Native Americans have experienced a world that has changed radically from the one into which they were born. Many of them were the first in their families to forsake ancestral

Elders, like John Burnsides, Navajo, *right*, remain honored and respected for the wisdom and skills that they have acquired and pass on to a younger generation. The old act as an island of information and stability within the troubled sea of contemporary culture. Their reassertion of traditional values helps embattled groups confront the troubling toll of present-day problems. As living examples of survival, endurance, tranquility, and harmony, the elderly are role models that no social agency could hope to invent.

A young member of the Aragon family of Acoma Pueblo, *above,* combines the old with the new, creating an imaginative Acoma pottery hot-air balloon, seen in his family's booth at Santa Fe's Indian Market.

homelands in order to fight in foreign wars. They had to confront the very real barrier of language that so often made them seem like foreigners in their own land. Many were forced to leave their parents at an early age, literally kidnapped into a terrifying world of the Indian boarding school where they were made to give up their language, dress, and customs. From the trauma of difficult early childhood experiences came not so much anger or bitterness, but rather a thankfulness for who they were and where they had come from.

There is no doubt that some of these experiences have taken an enormous toll upon Native American communities. High rates of accidental death, substance abuse, and suicide are among the legacies of the demands of the 20th century upon the first Americans. But beyond the despair of some is the determination and belief of many. These rescuers are determined that language should not be lost, that ritual is sacred, that lore should endure, and that the legacy of all that has come before should be remembered. "It is good that there is one old man who can show you all these things."

Douglas Glenmore, Cheyenne, and his grandson make music with traditional instruments in their home in Busby, Montana, *right.* Like many older generation Native Americans, Glenmore practices many talents, making parfleche bags, drums, and flutes.

THE CHILDREN

The Native children of North America can look to an inheritance that is second to none. With a genetic and cultural heritage of many thousands of years, their young lives represent a spirit of renewal and hope that is the best that mankind has to offer. Their faces seem to reflect the many millenniums of their ancestors' lives upon the planet, their wonderful contribution to human history, and the promise for greatness still to come. In this package of new life, winsome and eager, are the legacy of the past and the hope of the future.

At the children's creative workshop of the Sixth-Nation Reserve in Brantford, Ontario, Mohawk children learn art and crafts skills from their elders. Leatherwork, beading, pottery, stone carving, and the making of cornhusk dolls are all taught by community members.

NATIVE AMERICAN RESOURCES

SITES, MONUMENTS, AND MUSEUMS

ALASKA

Alaska State Museum
Whittier Street
Juneau, AK 99811
(907) 465-2901
Indian and Eskimo artifacts of the Aleut, Athapaskan, and Indians of the Northwest Coast; items relating to native life in Juneau.

Anchorage Museum of History and Art
121 West 7th Avenue
Anchorage, AK 99501
(907) 264-4326
Prehistoric artifacts including Alaskan cultures; exhibits of early Alaskan artists, contemporary arts and crafts.

Museum of the Arctic
NANA Regional Corporation
Box 49
Kotzebue, AK 99752
(907) 442-3301
Dioramas of the Arctic environment and animal sea life; cultural exhibits

Sheldon Jackson Museum
104 College Drive
Box 479
Sitka, AK 99835
(907) 747-8981
Houses 5,000 Alaska Eskimo, Aleut, Athabaskan, Tlingit, and Haida objects collected before 1900.

Sitka National Historical Park
P.O. Box 738
Sitka, AK 99835
(907) 747-6281
Site of the last major Tlingit Indian resistance to Russian colonization; Haida and Tlingit totem poles, crafts exhibited.

Southeast Alaska Indian Culture Center
P.O. Box 944
Sitka, AK 99835
(907) 747-6281
Located at Sitka National Historical Park. Skilled native artisans demonstrate traditional crafts.

Totem Heritage Center
601 Deermount
Ketchikan, AK 99901
(907) 225-5900
Totem pole collection, craft programs, and workshops of Northwest Coast Indian art.

ARIZONA

The Amerind Foundation
P.O. Box 248
Dragoon, AZ 85609
(602) 586-3666
Excellent Apache basket collection. Large collection of ethnographic beadwork.

Arizona State Museum
University of Arizona
Tucson, AZ 85721
(602) 621-6281
Southwestern archeology museum; Indian crafts and museum. Related items for sale.

Canyon de Chelly National Monument
P.O. Box 588
Chinle, AZ 86503
(602) 674-5436
Ruins of Indian villages built between A.D. 350 and 1300 at the base of sheer red cliffs and in canyon wall caves. Modern Navajo Indians live and farm here.

Casa Grande National Monument
P.O. Box 518
Coolidge, AZ 85228
(602) 723-3172
Ruins of a massive four-story building constructed by Indians who farmed the Gila Valley 600 years ago.

The Fred Harvey Co.
El Tovar Hotel
Grand Canyon, AZ 86023
(602) 527-2122
When the Santa Fe Railroad first reached the Grand Canyon, construction began on a first-class hotel. The El Tovar was opened in 1905, named after the Spanish explorer Pedro de Tovar, who led the first expedition to Hopi Indian country. The Fred Harvey Company had been building and operating facilities for food and rest along the Santa Fe route since 1876, a tradition maintained to this day.

The Heard Museum
22 East Monte Vista Road
Phoenix, AZ 85004
(602) 252-8848
Outstanding collection of works by American Indians. Reference material, library open to the public. Publishes quarterly magazine, *Native Peoples.*

Hubbell Trading Post National Historic Site
P.O. Box 150
Ganado, AZ 86505
(602) 755-3254
Active trading post illustrates the influence of reservation traders on the Indians' way of life.

Montezuma Castle National Monument
P.O. Box 219
Camp Verde, AZ 86322
(602) 567-3322
One of the best-preserved cliff dwellings in the United States.

Museum of Northern Arizona
Fort Valley Road
Route 4, Box 720
Flagstaff, AZ 86001
(602) 774-5211
Artifacts of prehistoric American Indian art. In June, July, and August, exhibits and sales of Zuni, Hopi, and Navajo artists including pottery, paintings, sculptures, and jewelry; in July and August, Navajo Artists' Exhibition/Sale of contemporary and traditional jewelry, pottery, sand paintings, basketry, and weavings. Artist demonstrations with each exhibition. Monthly expeditions into back country of the Colorado Plateau,

Navajo Tribal Museum
Box 308, Highway 264
Window Rock, AZ 86515
(602) 871-6673 & 6675
Museum of Navajo history; fine arts, photo archives. Related items for sale.

Pueblo Grande Museum
4619 East Washington Street
Phoenix, AZ 85034
(602) 275-3452
Findings from archeological digs and ethnographic material from the greater Southwest. Tour of platform mounds of ancient Hohokam sites. Annual Indian Market on the second weekend in December.

Tonto National Museum
Highway 88
Roosevelt, AZ 85545
(602) 467-2241
Well-preserved cliff dwellings. Park museum houses clothing, tools, weapons, and pottery of the Salado, prehistoric Indians of the region.

Tuzigoot National Monument
P.O. Box 68
Clarkdale, AZ 86324
(602) 634-5564
Ruins of a large Indian pueblo that flourished in the Verde Valley between 1100 and 1450.

Walnut Canyon National Monument
Walnut Canyon Road
Flagstaff, AZ 86004-9705
(602) 526-3367
Cliff dwellings built by Pueblo Indians about 800 years ago.

Wupatki National Monument
H.C. 33, Box 444A
Flagstaff, AZ 86004
(602) 527-7040
Ruins of red sandstone pueblos built by farming Indians about 1065. The modern Hopi Indians are believed to be partly descended from these people.

CALIFORNIA

Charles W. Bowers Museum
2002 North Main Street
Santa Ana, CA 92706
(714) 972-1900
Native American basketry and prehistoric Southwestern Indian ceramics on permanent exhibition. Collections of 19th- and 20th-century American Indian artifacts. Seminars, community festivals, films, and a Mexican/American Arts Council.

Lava Beds National Monument
P.O. Box 867
Tulelake, CA 96134
(916) 667-2282
Volcanic activity has created an incredibly rugged landscape—a natural fortress used by the Indians in the Modoc Indian War, 1872–73.

Marin Museum
2200 Novato Boulevard
Novato, CA 94947
(209) 897-4064
Photographic material related to California Indians; archeological, ethnographic, and archival collections ranging from Alaska to Peru and pertaining to the Indians of Marin County and Western Americas. Annual American Indian Trade Feast.

San Diego Museum of Man
1350 El Prado, Balboa Park
San Diego, CA 92101
(619) 239-2001 (museum);
298-4114 (fair)
Ethnological and archeological collections pertaining to people of the Americas; arts and crafts items for sale. Annual Indian Fair in June, with crafts and arts of over 20 Southwestern peoples; songs and dances.

Southwest Museum
234 Museum Drive Avenue, #43
Exit 110 on Pasadena Freeway
Los Angeles, CA 90042
(213) 221-2164
Collection of half a million Indian artifacts, including culture of prehistoric and historic North, Central, and South American Indians. Collector's Club; Annual Indian Art Show and Sale.

University of California
Robert H. Lowie Museum of Anthropology
103 Kroeber Hall
Berkeley, CA 94720
(415) 642-3681
Collection of archeological and ethnographic specimens from the Americas, Oceania, Europe, Asia, and Africa.

COLORADO

Adams State College Museum
Richardson Hall
Alamosa, CO 81102
(303) 589-7121
Collection includes Pueblo Indian artifacts, pottery, and Navajo weavings.

Bent's Old Fort National Historic Site
35110 Highway 194 East
La Junta, CO 81050-9523
(917) 384-2800
The fort was an Indian trading center and a center of civilization on the Santa Fe Trail.

Colorado National Monument
Fruita, CO 81521
(303) 858-3617
Walled canyons, towering monoliths, strange formations, dinosaur fossils, formations, and remains of prehistoric Indian cultures.

Denver Art Museum
100 West 14th Avenue Parkway
Denver, CO 80204
(303) 575-2295
Native arts collections from the United States, Canada, Africa, and Oceania.

Hovenweep National Monument
c/o Mesa Verde National Park
Mesa Verde National Park, CO 81330
(303) 529-4461
(Also in Utah)
Groups of towers, pueblos, and cliff dwellings built by pre-Columbian Indians.

Mesa Verde National Park
Mesa Verde National Park, CO 81330
(303) 529-4461
Notable and well-preserved pre-Columbian cliff dwellings and other works of early man.

CONNECTICUT

American Indian Archaeological Institute
Curtis Road, off Route 199
P.O. Box 260
Washington, CT 06793
(203) 868-0518
Prehistoric and historic artifacts primarily from Connecticut and the Northeastern United States. Indian habitat, trail, reconstructed Indian village, and arboretum of plants used by Indians 10,000 years ago. Native American studies program.

DISTRICT OF COLUMBIA

Smithsonian Institution
100 Jefferson Drive SW
Washington, DC 20560
(202) 357-1300
National museum collections.

U.S. Department of the Interior Museum
18th and C Streets NW
Washington, DC 20240
(202) 343-3477 and 343-2743
Collections from cultures of the American Indian, the Eskimo, Micronesia, Virgin Islands, and Guam. Handicrafts, artifacts, and paintings.

FLORIDA

Big Cypress National Preserve
Star Route, Box 110
Ochopee, FL 33943
(813) 262-1066
Adjoins the northwest section of Everglades National Park. Ancestral home of the Seminole and Miccosukee Indians.

Collier-Seminole State Park
Route 4, Box 848
Naples, FL 33961
(813) 394-3997
Some of the final campaigns of the Second Seminole War were conducted near here. A park named for B. Collier, pioneer developer, and for the Seminole Indians who still live nearby.

Crystal River State Archeological Site
3400 North Museum Place
Crystal River, FL 32629
(904) 795-3817
State museum. Artifacts of pre-Columbian Indians.

Museum of Art, Inc.
1 East Las Olas Boulevard
Fort Lauderdale, FL 33301
(305) 525-5500
Pre-Columbian and historic American Indian and Oceanic stone and wood carvings; ceramics, basketry, and textiles. Seminars and lectures; arts festivals.

Museum of Science
3280 South Miami Avenue
Miami, FL 33129
(305) 854-4247
Major collection of Florida Indian artifacts.

GEORGIA

Kalomaki Mounds State Park Museum
Route 1
Blakely, GA 31723
(912) 723-3398
Historic 13th-century Indian burial mound and village site. Indian artifacts, excavated mound, and Mississippian mound complex.

Ocmulgee National Monument
1207 Emery Highway
Macon, GA 31201
(912) 752-8257
Traces of more than 10,000 years of Southeastern prehistory from Ice Age Paleo Indians to the historic Creek Confederacy. Massive temple mounds of a Mississippian Indian ceremonial complex A.D. 900–1100.

IDAHO

Nez Percé National Historical Park
P.O. Box 93
Spalding, ID 83551
(208) 843-2261
Preserves, commemorates, and interprets the history and culture of the Nez Percé Indian.

ILLINOIS

Field Museum of Natural History
Roosevelt Road, at Lake Shore Drive
Chicago, IL 60605
(312) 922-9410
Major Indian artifacts collection.

INDIANA

Eiteljorg Museum of American Indian and Western Art
500 West Washington Street
White River State Park
Indianapolis, IN 46204
(317) 636-9378
The newest museum, opening in 1989, dedicated to Western Americana, with a gallery devoted to Native American material culture.

Museum store, the White River Trader, focuses on sale of Native American art.

Museum of Indian Heritage
6040 De Long Road
Eagle Creek Park
Indianapolis, IN 46254
(317) 293-4488
Collections of archeology, ethnology, history, and contemporary life dealing with the American Indian; arts and crafts for sale.

IOWA

Effigy Mounds National Monument
R.R. 1, Box 25A
Harpers Ferry, IA 52146
(319) 873-3491
Outstanding examples of prehistoric American Indian mounds, some in the shape of birds and bears.

KANSAS

Fort Larned National Historic Site
Route 3
Larned, KS 67550
(316) 285-6911
Military outpost established midway along the Santa Fe Trail in 1859, to protect the mail and travelers. Fort served as a bureau for the Indian Agency during much of the 1860s, and was a key military base of operations during the Indian War of 1868–69.

MINNESOTA

Grand Portage National Monument
P.O. Box 666
Grand Marais, MN 55604
(218) 475-2592
This 9-mile portage was a vital link on one of the principal routes for Indians, explorers, missionaries, and fur traders heading for the Northwest. Grand Portage post of the North West Company has been reconstructed.

Pipestone National Monument
P.O. Box 727
Pipestone, MN 56164
(507) 825-5463
From this quarry, Indians obtained materials for making pipes used in ceremonies. Collection of Indian ceremonial pipes and pipestone objects; Indian-made pipes and beadwork for sale.

MONTANA

Big Hole National Battlefield
P.O. Box 237
Wisdom, MT 59761
(406) 689-3136
Nez Percé Indians and U.S. Army troops fought here in 1877, part of a long struggle to confine the Nez Percé and other Indians to reservations.

C. M. Russell Museum
400 13th Street
Great Falls, MT 59045
(406) 727-8787
Log cabin studio of C. M. Russell adjacent to museum commemorates life of the Montana artist. C. M. Russell Art Auction in late March; 3-day event featuring historic exhibitions of Western art, auctions, and seminars.

Custer Battlefield National Monument
P.O. Box 39
Crow Agency, MT 59022
(406) 638-2621
The Battle of the Little Big Horn between 12 companies of the U.S. Seventh Cavalry and the Sioux and Northern Cheyenne Indians was fought here June 25–26, 1876.

Museum of the Plains Indians and Craft Center
P.O. Box 400
Browning, MT 59417
(406) 338-2230
Collections of Northern Plains Indians ceremonial arts, contemporary Indian arts, murals, dioramas, and craft shop. Administered by Indian Arts and Crafts Board, U.S. Interior Department.

NEW MEXICO

Aztec Ruins National Monument
P.O. Box 640
Aztec, NM 87410
(505) 334-6174
Ruins of a large Pueblo Indian community.

Bandelier National Monument
Los Alamos, NM 87544
45 miles northwest of Santa Fe
(505) 672-3861
Large site of a prehistoric Indian ruin. Museum and gift shop, self-directed walks, camping, hiking, picnicking.

Chaco Culture National Historical Park
Star Route 4, Box 6500
Bloomfield, NM 87413
(505) 988-6727
The canyon, with hundreds of small ruins, contains 13 major Indian ruins unsurpassed in the United States, representing the highest point of Pueblo pre-Columbian civilization.

El Morro National Monument
Ramah, NM 87321
(505) 783-4226
Pre-Columbian petroglyphs and Pueblo Indian ruins.

Gadsden Museum
Barker Road and Highway 28
Mesilla, NM 88046
(505) 526-6293
Individually owned museum with collections of Indian artifacts from the Southwest.

Gila Cliff Dwellings National Monument
Route 11, Box 100
Silver City, NM 88061
(505) 536-9344
Well-preserved cliff dwellings inhabited from about 1280 to the early 1300s.

Institute of American Indian Arts Museum
1369 Cerrillos Road
Santa Fe, NM 87501
(505) 988-6281
Exhibits of Native American arts and culture; slides of contemporary Indian art from over 100 Tribes.

Kit Carson House
One block east of Taos Plaza
Taos, NM 87571
(505) 758-4741
Home and museum of the famous Mountain Man; exhibits on prehistoric Indians and archeology, Spanish history, and early Anglo-American culture. Registered as a National Historic Landmark.

Maxwell Museum of Anthropology
University of New Mexico
Albuquerque, NM 87131
(505) 277-4404
Anthropology museum, archeology, ethnology, specialized Southwest collections, weaving, kachina dolls, Mimbres Pueblo pottery, American Indian basketry, musical instruments. Archeological expressions of the ancient inhabitants of this region as well as utilitarian and artistic work of more recent peoples. Holdings from other areas of the New World.

Mescalero Apache Cultural Center
P.O. Box 175
Mescalero, NM 88340
(505) 671-4495
Operates Inn of the Mountain Gods lodge.

Millicent Rogers Museum
4 miles north of Taos on Highway 3
Taos, NM 87571
(505) 758-2462
Fine collection of Native American and Hispanic art. Founded in memory of Millicent Rogers, museum is a repository for Navajo, Pueblo, and Hispanic cultural materials.

Museum of Indian Arts and Culture
710 Camino Lejo
Santa Fe, NM 87501
(505) 827-8000
A new museum housing the State of New Mexico's vast collections of Indian arts.

Pecos National Monument
P.O. Drawer 11
Pecos, NM 87552
(505) 757-6032
Ruins of the ancient pueblo of Pecos and the remains of two Spanish missions, one built in the 17th and the other in the 18th century.

Red Rock Museum
Red Rock State Park
Church Rock, NM 87311 (near Gallup)
(505) 722-6196
Collections of crafts and artifacts of prehistoric Anasazi and historic Navajo, Hopi, Zuni, Rio Grande Pueblos, and Apache Indians.

Roswell Museum of Art Center
100 West 11th Street
Roswell, NM 88201
(505) 624-6744
Collection of American Indian and Western art. Outstanding examples of Indian quill and beadwork.

Salinas National Monument
Box 496
Mountainair, NM 87036
(505) 847-2585
Preserves and interprets the best examples of 17th-century Spanish Franciscan mission churches and convents remaining in the United States and three of the largest Pueblo Indian villages, representing cultural traditions extending at least 7,000 years into the past.

Wheelwright Museum of the American Indian
704 Camino Lejo
Box 5153
Santa Fe, NM 87502
(505) 982-4636
Cofounded by Mary Cabot Wheelwright and Hasteen Klah to promote understanding between Indian and non-Indian people. Features exhibits of contemporary and historic Indian art; innovative programs including travel outside the Southwest. Quarterly publication, *The Messenger*.

NEW YORK

Akwesane Museum
Route 37, State Highway 37
Hogansburg, NY 13655
(518) 358-2461
Artifacts, baskets, stone carvings, paintings, wampum belts, bead and quillwork. Gift shop sells baskets of light ash and sweetgrass, beadwork, books.

American Museum of Natural History
Central Park West at 79th Street
New York, NY 10024
(212) 769-5100
Extensive collection of Northwest Coast Indian art.

Brooklyn Museum
200 Eastern Parkway
Brooklyn, NY 11238
(718) 638-5000
Collections of American Indian art; artifacts collected in southwestern California and the Northwest Coast on permanent exhibition.

Iroquois Indian Museum
Box 158 North Main Street
Department DB
Schoharie, NY 12157
(518) 295-8553
Features today's Iroquois artists. Selected silver jewelry, pottery, antler and stone carvings, baskets, beadwork, leather and cornhusk work.

Museum of the American Indian
Heye Foundation
155th Street and Broadway
New York, NY 10032
(212) 283-2420
Collections include Eskimo culture, American Indian archeology and ethnology from North, Central, and South America and the Caribbean. Museum features prehistoric and historic Indian culture, has collection of textiles, sculpture, decorative arts, and costumes. Film and video collection on and by Native Americans.

Native American Centre for Living Arts, Inc.
25 Rainbow Mall
Niagara Falls, NY 14801
(716) 284-2427
Collections of Native American art; contemporary Indian art from Mexico, U.S., and Canada; Native American archives and iconography.

Seneca-Iroquois National Museum
P.O. Box 442, Broad Street Extension
Salamanca, NY 14779
(716) 945-1738
Collects, preserves, displays, and interprets to the general public objects, artifacts, and national cultural treasures related to the Iroquois people, especially the Seneca Nation. Changing exhibits show various aspects of Seneca and Iroquois life.

NORTH CAROLINA

Museum of the Cherokee Indian
U.S. Highway 441 North
P.O. Box 770-A
Cherokee, NC 28719
(704) 497-3481
Owned by Eastern Band of Cherokee Indians. Collections of relics, Indian artifacts; conducts research on Cherokee culture, language, and history.

NORTH DAKOTA

Knife River Indian Villages National Historic Site
R.R. 1, Box 168
Stanton, ND 58571
(701) 745-3309
Remnants of historic and prehistoric American Indian villages, last occupied in 1845 by the Hidatsa and Mandan. Site contains an array of artifacts of Plains Indian culture.

OHIO

Mound City Group National Monument
16062 State Route 104
Chillicothe, OH 45601
(614) 774-1125
Twenty-three burial mounds of Hopewell Indians (200 B.C.–A.D. 500). Yields of copper breastplates, tools, obsidian blades, shells, ornaments of grizzly bear teeth, and stone pipes carved as birds and animals provide insights into the ceremonial customs of these prehistoric people.

OKLAHOMA

Center of the American Indian
2100 Northeast 52nd Street
Kirkpatrick Center
Oklahoma City, OK 73111
(405) 427-5461
Outstanding collection of art and cultural materials from prehistoric to contemporary, representing several tribes of American Indians.

Cherokee National Museum (Heritage Center)
P.O. Box 515
Tahlequah, OK 74464
(918) 456-6007
Cherokee heritage museum, site of ancient village. Annual Trail of Tears Art Show and Outdoor Drama of Cherokees torn from their ancestral homes in Eastern highlands and forced into territory now State of Oklahoma. Show attracts over 140 artists from 41 different groups.

Chickasaw Council House Museum
Court House Square, P.O. Box 717
Tishomingo, OK 73460
(405) 371-3351
First Council House built and used by the Chickasaws, housed inside museum building. Collection of items relating to lives of Chickasaws in the Territory of Oklahoma. Exhibits highlight Chickasaw culture from 1540 to the present.

Choctaw Council House Historical Museum
Route 1, Box 105-3A
Tuskohoma, OK 74574
(918) 569-4465
Building was once the capital of the Choctaw Nation. Collection of artifacts, paintings, and photographs.

Creek Council House and Museum
Town Square
Okmulgee, OK 74447
(918) 756-2324
Creek Indian artifacts, art, archeology exhibits. Okmulgee pioneer history.

The Five Civilized Tribes Museum
Agency Hill, Honor Heights Drive
Muskogee, OK 74401
(918) 683-1701
Traditional Indian art and authentic Indian artifacts, representing Cherokee, Chickasaw, Choctaw, Creek, and Seminole peoples. Building is original structure of the Union Indian Agency, built 1875.

Indian City, USA
P.O. Box 695
2 miles southeast of Anadarko
Anadarko, OK 73005
(405) 247-5661
Life-size village. Guided tours, Indian dancing.

Kiowa Tribal Museum
P.O. Box 369
Carnegie, OK 73015
(405) 654-2300 ext. 217
Artifacts, artwork, and resource materials of the Kiowas.

Memorial Indian Museum
2nd and Allen streets
Broken Bow, OK 74728
(405) 584-6531
Indian artifacts from prehistoric to modern times, including a large collection of prehistoric Caddo Indian pottery, prehistoric Indian skeletal remains, and early beadwork.

Osage Tribal Museum
Osage Agency Campus
Grandview Avenue
Pawhuska, OK 74056
(918) 287-2495, ext. 280
Artifacts of Osages, art gallery. Rare photographs of early Osages.

Philbrook Art Center, Inc.
2727 South Rockford Road
Tulsa, OK 74114
(918) 749-7941
Collection of American Indian baskets, pottery, costumes, and paintings. Also has Indian library.

Seminole Nation Museum
P.O. Box 1532
524 South Wewoka Avenue
Wewoka, OK 74884
(405) 257-5580
Mementos belonging to Chief Stande Waite; photographs of early settlers, Indians and freedmen; Seminole heritage artifacts. Art gallery; arts and crafts of Seminole and Creek Indians for sale.

Southern Plains Indian Museum
Box 749
Anadarko, OK 73005
(405) 247-6221
Permanent exhibit presents diversity of historic arts of peoples of western Oklahoma; one gallery devoted to creative works of outstanding contemporary Native American artists and craftsmen. Museum shop operated by Oklahoma Indian Arts and Crafts Cooperative offers wide variety of beadwork, featherwork, and dance costumes and accessories. Sponsors Annual American Indian Exposition in August.

Spiro Mounds Archaeological State Park
Route 2, Box 339AA
Spiro, OK 74959
(918) 962-2062
Features artifacts on life and culture of prehistoric Indians discovered through excavation of burial mounds in 1930.

Thomas Gilcrease Institute of American History and Art
1400 Gilcrease Museum Road
Tulsa, OK 74127
(918) 582-3124
Collections of the cultures of Five Civilized Tribes; American Indian artifacts; documents and graphics of the westward movement in the United States.

OREGON

Museum of Natural History
University of Oregon
Eugene, OR 97403
(503) 686-3024
Collection features Northwest Coast Indian masks and basketry, prehistoric artifacts from Eastern Oregon, Navajo blankets.

SOUTH DAKOTA

The Heritage Center
Red Cloud Indian School
Pine Ridge, SD 57770
(605) 867-5491
Indian art museum. Paintings by American Indian artists, star quilt, beadwork, quill and pottery collection. Sioux bead and quillwork for sale.

Sioux Indian Museum
Box 1504
Rapid City, SD 57709
(605) 348-0557 or 8834
Exhibits creative works of Sioux craftsmen and other Native American artists; has permanent collection of historic Sioux arts. Craft products from reservations of South Dakota, North Dakota, Montana, and Minnesota for sale in Tipi Shop. Administered and operated by Indian Crafts Board.

TEXAS

Alibates Flint Quarries National Monument
c/o Lake Meredith Recreation Area
P.O. Box 1438
Fritch, TX 79036
(806) 857-3151
For more than 10,000 years Indians dug agatized dolomite from quarries here to make projectile points, knives, scrapers, and other tools.

UTAH

Canyonlands National Park
125 West 200 South
Moab, UT 84532
(801) 259-7164
In this geological wonder, rocks, spires, and mesas rise more than 7,800 feet. Contains petroglyphs left by Indians about 1,000 years ago.

Natural Bridges National Monument
Box 1
Lake Powell, UT 84533
(801) 259-5174
Three natural bridges carved out of sandstone, including the second and third largest in the world. Under one bridge are ancient Anasazi Indian rock art and ruins.

WASHINGTON

Daybreak Star Arts Center
P.O. Box 99253
Seattle, WA 98199
(206) 285-4425
Nonprofit organization sells baskets, bags, masks, sculptures, silver jewelry, paintings, Navajo rugs. Commissions accepted. Sponsors Seafair Days Powwow in July, with dance competitions, banner contest, arts and crafts exhibition and sale.

Makah Cultural and Research Center
P.O. Box 95
Neah Bay, WA 98357
(206) 645-2711
Cultural center houses Makah Indian artifacts found in archeological site covered by a mudslide 500 years ago; some items over 2,000 years old. Museum contains replicas of 60-foot cedar longhouse; oceangoing canoes used by Makah Indians for whale and seal hunting.

Museum of Native American Culture
East 200 Cataldo Street
Spokane, WA 99220
(509) 326-4550
Artifacts, paintings, and documents representing many Indian groups.

Thomas Burke Memorial
Washington State Museum
University of Washington
17th Avenue, northeast entrance
Seattle, WA 98195
(206) 543-5590
Exhibitions of Northwest Indians and artifacts of peoples of the Pacific rim.

Tillicum Village
Northwest Coast Indian Cultural Center
Blake Island Marine State Park
Take boat from Pier 56, Seattle
(206) 329-5700
Ancestral fishing camp of the Suquamish Indians. Wood carvings and typical Indian foods.

WISCONSIN

Arts and Crafts Cultural Center
P.O. Box 529
Bayfield, WI 54814
(715) 779-5858
Products available include wood carvings, beadwork, paintings, and birchbark items produced by Lake Superior Band of Chippewas.

WYOMING

Buffalo Bill Historic Center
On U.S. 14/16/20
720 Sheridan Avenue
Cody, WY 82414
(307) 587-4771
Whitney Gallery of Western Arts; Buffalo Bill Museum; Plains Indian Museum; Winchester Arms Museum. Plains Museum has extensive collection of ceremonial items and beadwork, dress and weaponry of the Sioux, Blackfeet, Cheyenne, Shoshone, Crow, and Arapaho.

CANADA

British Columbia Provincial Museum
675 Belleville Street
Victoria, BC V8V 1X4
(604) 387-3701; 604-3014 for message
Exhibits and interprets collections about the human and natural history of British Columbia. Indian cultural heritage exhibits include textiles, totem poles, masks, and carvings.

Kwagiulth Museum
Box 8
Quathiaski Cove, BC V0P 1N0
(604) 285-3733
In Cape Mudge Village, Quadra Island, British Columbia. Preserves history and traditions of the Kwagiulth people. Potlatch Collection features sacred ceremonial objects and cedar bark regalia.

Museum of Northern British Columbia
First Avenue and McBride Street
P.O. Box 669
Prince Rupert, BC V8J 3S1
(604) 624-3207
Objects from Northwest Coast Indian culture. Displays explain prehistoric lifestyles of the Coastal Indians. Modern Indian carving done on museum grounds.

U'Mista Cultural Center
P.O. Box 253
Alert Bay, BC V0N 1A0
(604) 974-5403
Collection of masks, copper items, and other gifts from Indian potlatches, the gift-giving ceremonies that mark such important occasions as the naming of children, marriage, and death. In Alert Bay Indian fishing village, which contains a number of totem poles.

University of British Columbia Museum of Anthropology
6393 Northwest Marine Drive
Vancouver, BC V6T 1W5
(604) 228-3825 (taped message)
(604) 228-5087 (business)
World's finest collection of Northwest Coast Indian art. Includes huge totem poles, replicas of Indian longhouse.

Woodland Cultural Educational Center
184 Mohawk Street
Brantford, ON N3T 5V6
(519) 759-2650
Research library has extensive collection of woodland titles, artist files, and archival materials. Educational program produces curriculum materials for Native studies. Collections of prehistoric pottery, wampum, basketry, clothing, musical instruments, and contemporary art.

ORGANIZATIONS, PUBLICATIONS, AND GUIDES

ALASKA

Alaska Native Arts and Crafts Association
425 D Street
Anchorage, AK 99501
(907) 274-2932
A nonprofit marketing association for Alaskan Natives, selling ivory carvings, whalebone sculpture, masks, baskets of birchbark, grass, and baleen.

Alaska Native Arts and Crafts Center of Fairbanks Alaska
1603 College Road
Fairbanks, AK 99701
(907) 456-2323
Retail sales of Native-tanned moose and caribou skin purses, pouches, gloves, slippers, dolls, baskets, parkas and fur hats, masks, ivory carvings, jewelry of shell, beads, feathers, and porcupine quills.

Institute of Alaska Native Arts
P.O. Box 80583
Fairbanks, AK 99708
(907) 479-8473 or 4436
An organization that supports Alaska Native art and education, both traditional and contemporary.

ARIZONA

American Indian Art Magazine
7314 East Osborn Drive
Scottsdale, AZ 85251
(602) 994-5445
Primary resource for collectors. Lists events and shows. Book reviews and museum events. Quarterly.

Arizona Highways
2039 West Lewis Avenue
Phoenix, AZ 85009
(602) 258-1000
Published monthly by Arizona Department of Transportation. Outstanding photography of state's beauty; in-depth articles on Anasazi ruins, Navajo land, and Hopis; book reviews.

ATLATL
Publication of a Native American Arts Service Organization
402 West Roosevelt
Phoenix, AZ 85003
(602) 253-2731
Lists Indian markets, exhibits, and events, also workshops and presentations.

Hopi Arts and Crafts Silvercraft Cooperative Guild
P.O. Box 36
Second Mesa, AZ 86043
(602) 734-2463
Sells Hopi overlay jewelry, coiled and wicker baskets and plaques, pottery, kachina dolls, cloth Hopi dolls, textiles.

National Native America Cooperation
Box 30
San Carlos, AZ 85550
(602) 475-2229
Cooperative representing 1,500 artists from 60 tribes. Publishes Native American Directory with dates of powwows and celebrations, lists of national Indian organizations, craft guilds, cultural centers, urban Indian centers, and Indian media.

Native Peoples Magazine
Media Concepts Group, Inc.
1833 North Third Street
Phoenix, AZ 85004-1502
(602) 252-2236
Color photographs and relevant contemporary articles on Native peoples enliven this new quarterly publication.

Native Seeds/Search
3950 West Northwest York Drive
Tucson, AZ 85745
(602) 327-9123
Publishes Seedhead News, a seed listing and catalogue of seeds books.

Papago Tribal Arts and Crafts Cooperative Guild
Box 837
Sells, AZ 85634
(602) 383-2221, ext. 380
Papago craftspersons produce coiled yucca basketry and miniature baskets of horsehair.

CALIFORNIA

American Indian Contemporary Crafts
Monadnock Building
685 Market Street, Suite 270
San Francisco, CA 94105-4212
(415) 495-7600
Dedicated to promotion and advancement of American Indian art. Encourages artistic tradition and expression as a vital aspect of Native culture; provides information about Indian art to the general public. Publishes Native Vision, a bimonthly providing information on national and local art exhibitions and events.

American Indian Culture and Research Journal
American Indian Studies Center
3220 Campbell Hall
University of California
405 Hilgard Avenue
Los Angeles, CA 90024-1548
(213) 825-4777 or 825-7315
Scholarly quarterly providing an interdisciplinary forum for significant contributions of knowledge regarding American Indians. Reviews books.

California
11601 Wilshire Boulevard
Los Angeles, CA 90025
(213) 479-6511
Statewide guide to arts events, with a travel section and book reviews. Published monthly.

Masterkey: Anthropology of the Americas
Southwest Museum
Box 128
Los Angeles, CA 90042
(213) 221-2163
Sophisticated articles and book reviews pertaining to California and Indian cultures of the South and West.

Sacramento Indian Center
Arts and Crafts
2616 K Street
Sacramento, CA 95816
(916) 442-0593
In California State Indian Museum Building. Sells leatherwork, baskets, silver and turquoise jewelry, paintings.

Sunset Magazine
80 Willow Road
Menlo Park, CA 94025
(415) 321-3600
Travel guide by regions. Lists special events.

COLORADO

Western Art Digest
812 South Tejon Street
Colorado Springs, CO 80903
Published bimonthly by Artists of the Rockies and the Golden West, Inc. Museum collections and new artists articles, book reviews, museum calendar and events.

CONNECTICUT

American Indian Archaeological Institute (AIAI)
Route 199, Box 260
Washington, CT 06793
(203) 868-0518
Preserves and interprets information about Native American peoples of the Northeastern Woodlands area of the United States. Sponsors archeological training sessions, teacher workshops, summer youth programs, lectures, and film festivals.

DISTRICT OF COLUMBIA

Indian Arts and Crafts Board
Room 4004
U.S. Department of Interior
Washington, DC 20240
(202) 343-2773
Works with persons operating Indian arts and crafts businesses. Publishes directory of Indian-owned and -operated businesses marketing authentic contemporary Native American arts and crafts and representing cooperatives and Native-operated enterprises.

National Geographic Traveler
P.O. Box 37054
Washington, DC 20036
(202) 828-5485
An educational travel resource with quarterly issues. Events listed by regions of United States, Canada, and Mexico.

IDAHO

Nez Percé Arts and Crafts Guild
P.O. Box 205
Lapwai, ID 83540
Nez Percé crafts featuring beadwork, buckskin, and cornhusk basketry.

MARYLAND

Daybreak
P.O. Box 98
Highland, MD 20777-0098
(301) 854-0499
Published quarterly by a Native American collective dedicated to the preservation of Mother Earth and recognition for the cultural diversity of her inhabitants.

MONTANA

Blackfeet Crafts Association
On U.S. 89 in St. Mary
P.O. Box 51
Browning, MT 59417
Shop featuring beadwork in all mediums.

Chippewa Cree Crafts
Tribal Building
Rocky Boy Route
Box Elder, MT 59521
(406) 395-4478
Indian Women Cooperative featuring beadwork in all mediums. Catalogue and mail orders.

Northern Cheyenne Arts and Crafts Association
U.S. Route 212 and State Highway 315
Northern Cheyenne Indian Reservation
Lame Deer, MT 59043
(406) 477-6284
Sells beadwork and buckskin accessories.

Northern Plains Indian Crafts Association
P.O. Box E
Browning, MT 59417
(406) 338-5661
Sells buckskin vests, gloves, handbags, moccasins, beadwork.

NEW MEXICO

Artlist
Quick Trak Market Reports
P.O. Box 35552
Albuquerque, NM 87176
(505) 881-3246
Indian art prices at auction used by collectors, appraisers, galleries, museums, and libraries.

Eight Northern Indian Pueblos Council
P.O. Box 969
San Juan Pueblo, NM 87566
(505) 852-4265
Tesuque, Pojoaque, San Ildefonso, Santa Clara, Nambe, San Juan, Picuris, and Taos organized into Pueblo Council to sponsor art and craft show. Also publishes extensive visitors guide to individual villages including calendar of events, maps, and other information.

Eight Northern Pueblo Indian Artisans Guild
P.O. Box 1079
San Juan Pueblo, NM 87566
(505) 852-4283
Eight Northern Pueblos craftwork of drums, pottery, jewelry, kachinas, wood carvings.

Indian Arts and Crafts Association
Darrow Building
4215 Lead Avenue, SE
P.O. Box 40013
Albuquerque, NM 87108
(505) 265-9149
National nonprofit organization of Indian craftspeople, museums, dealers, collectors, and others committed to maintaining the image, marketing, and understanding of Indian handmade arts and crafts. Sponsors annual Arizona Wholesale Market for retailers.

Indian Market
Published by Southwestern Association on Indian Affairs
P.O. Box 1964
Santa Fe, NM 87501-1964
(505) 983-5220
Magazine concerned with Indian Market; Contains expert views on Indian art, history, and purchasing information.

Indian National Final Rodeo Commission
P.O. Box 1725
Albuquerque, NM 87103
(505) 898-2667
Sponsors annual Native American rodeo.

Indian Pueblo Cultural Center, Inc.
2401 12th Street NW
Albuquerque, NM 87102
(505) 843-7270 or 843-7271
Cultural and social gathering point for Pueblo Indians, with a wide range of activities year round. Provides educational resource for young people; collections and facilities serve as research basis for scholars, artists, and writers. Founded 1978.

The Indian Trader
Box 867
102 West Hill
Gallup, NM 87301
(505) 722-3493
Monthly magazine devoted to Western and Indian arts and crafts. Directory of Indian trading posts, galleries, and museums.

Institute of American Indian Arts
Museum Sales
1369 Cerrillos Road
Santa Fe, NM 87501
(505) 988-6281
A junior college which offers training in museum work. Student works of traditional painting, sculpture, printmaking, and beadwork for sale; also artwork of students and alumni.

Inter-Tribal Ceremonial Association
Box One
Church Rock, NM 87311
(505) 863-3896
An official agency of the State of New Mexico. Promotes virtues and beauty of traditional Indian cultures.

Native Plant Society of New Mexico
Santa Fe Chapter
P.O. Box 5917
Santa Fe, NM 87502
(505) 988-1702
Local chapters throughout the state offer a wide range of activities including field trips to identify native plants, workshops, plant sales, and monthly meetings. Landscaping, water conservation, and encouragement of interest in native plants.

New Mexico Magazine
Joseph M. Montoya Building
1100 St. Francis Drive
Santa Fe, NM 87503
(505) 827-0220
Articles relating to state. Lists events, especially Indian dances and exhibitions. Published monthly.

Oke Oweenge Arts and Crafts
P.O. Box 1095
San Juan Pueblo, NM 87566
Off U.S. Route 64, north of Espanola
(505) 852-2372
Features traditional costume items, carvings, dolls, beadwork, baskets, and paintings. Mail-order price list available; send self-addressed, stamped business envelope.

School of American Research
660 Garcia Street
Santa Fe, NM 87501
(505) 982-3583
Research Center open by appointment. Textiles and jewelry of Navajo and Pueblo Indians; Southwest Indian basketry, kachinas, and many ethnographic objects pertaining to Southwest Indian art.

Southwestern Association on Indian Affairs, Inc.
La Fonda Hotel
Santa Fe, NM 87501
(505) 983-5220
Sponsors annual Indian Market. Also meets throughout the year to discuss various aspects of Indian culture.

Zuni Craftsmen Cooperative Association
P.O. Box 426
Zuni, NM 87327
State Highway 53 at Zuni
(505) 782-4425
Located on Zuni Indian Reservation, where Zuni craftsmen produce fetishes, silver and turquoise jewelry, pottery, paintings, beadwork.

NEW YORK

Allegany Indian Arts and Crafts Cooperative
Haley Building, Jimersonton
Salamanca, NY 14779
(716) 945-1790
Cooperative features beadwork, masks, baskets, cornhusk dolls. Price list and mail order available.

Americana Magazine, Inc.
29 West 38th Street
New York, NY 10018
(212) 398-1550
Includes articles on American Indians, book reviews.

Native American Center for Living Arts, Inc.
25 Rainbow Mall
Niagara Falls, NY 14303
(716) 284-2427
Sells primarily Iroquois crafts including pottery, beadwork, cornhusk dolls, wall hangings, and carvings in bone and antler. Sponsors Annual Turtle Island Powwow held in May. Publishes *Turtle Quarterly Magazine* concerning Indian arts, myths, and folklore of the region.

NORTH CAROLINA

Qualla Arts and Crafts Mutual, Inc.
On Cherokee Indian Reservation at U.S. 441
P.O. Box 277
Cherokee, NC 28719
(704) 497-3103
Eastern Cherokee craftsmen cooperative produces basketry of various grasses, wood carvings, beadwork, metalwork, and pottery.

OKLAHOMA

Cherokee Advocate
P.O. Box 948
Tahlequah, OK 74465
Monthly magazine covers Cherokee Nation.

Oklahoma Indian Arts and Crafts Cooperative
P.O. Box 966
Anadarko, OK 73005
Southern Plains Indian museum shop. Displays and sells beaded moccasins, dance costume accessories and ornaments, war dance ensembles,

hand-decorated shirts, and original paintings by Southern Plains Indians

PENNSYLVANIA

Indian Artifacts Magazine
Department 1T
R.D. #1, Box 240
Turbotville, PA 17772
(717) 437-3698
Articles, pictures, historical and educational material on collecting, buying, and finding Indian artifacts and related items. Published quarterly.

TEXAS

Society for American Indian Studies and Research
P.O. Box 443
Hurst, TX 76053
(817) 281-3784
Organization, founded in 1974, which contributes to the preservation and publication of materials related to Indians in North and Middle America.

Southwest Art, Inc.
Box 460535
Houston, TX 77056-8535
(713) 850-0990
Color photos, book reviews, gallery guide; articles about historical and contemporary artists.

WASHINGTON

United Indians of All Tribes Foundation
Daybreak Star Arts Center
Discovery Park
P.O. Box 99253
Seattle, WA 98199
(206) 285-4425
A foundation advocating the interests of Native Americans. Promotes the development of Indian economic self-sufficiency and Indian arts and education.

WISCONSIN

Patch-Chee-Nunk Cooperative
Route 2, Box 247A
Wittenberg, WI 54499
(715) 253-2928
Cooperative of Great Lakes tribes. Products include featherwork, leatherwork, beadwork, and basketry.

CANADA

The Alberta Indian Arts and Crafts Society
#501, 10105–109 Street
Edmonton, AB T5J 1M0
(403) 426-2048
Society's 2,000 members create one-of-a-kind craft and art items: beadwork, moosehair, tufting, quillwork, and more. National craft shows in Edmonton and Calgary; summer arts festival in Edmonton.

SCHEDULES, CELEBRATIONS, AND EVENTS

Contact state offices of tourism for more information regarding schedules of events within the state and on Indian reservations.

ALABAMA

Annual Creek Indian Thanksgiving Day Powwow
Vickey Parker
Route 3, Box 243-A
Atmore, AL 36502
(205) 368-9136
Traditional dinner, entertainment, competitions, arts and crafts. Held at Creek Indian Tribal Center. Admission charge. Held on Thanksgiving Day.

ALASKA

All-Alaska Juried Art Exhibition
Anchorage Museum of History and Art
Anchorage, AK 99501-3696
(907) 264-4326
February.

Festival of Native Arts
University of Alaska
508 Gruenig Building
Fairbanks, AK 99775-1200
(907) 474-6603
Second weekend in March.

Potlatch Celebration of Spring
Fairbanks Native Association
310½ First Avenue
Fairbanks, AK 99701
(907) 452-1648
Third weekend in March.

Wood, Ivory, and Bone Native Arts Competition
Alaska State Council of Arts
619 Warehouse Avenue, #220
Anchorage, AK 99501
(907) 279-1558
Third weekend in February.

World Eskimo-Indian Olympics
P.O. Box 2433
Fairbanks, AK 99707
(907) 452-6646 or 456-2422
Annual celebration, featuring traditional athletic games and dances of the Arctic regions of the world. Held at Big Dipper Ice Arena. July. Admission charge.

ARIZONA

Annual Festival of Native American Arts
Coconino Center for the Arts
Box 296
Flagstaff, AZ 86002
(602) 779-6921
July 4–5 and August 1–2, from ten to five, Natives from the Four Corners area sell crafts and foods and perform their dances at Indian markets in Flagstaff.

Hopi Craftsmen Exhibition
Museum of Northern Arizona
Route 4, Box 720
Flagstaff, AZ 86001
(602) 774-5211
Baskets, rugs, kachinas, jewelry, toys, paintings, pots.

Navajoland Tourism Office
P.O. Box 308
Window Rock, AZ 86515
(602) 871-4941, ext. 1659
July—Fourth of July Celebration, rodeo. September—Navajo Nation Fair; parade, carnival, rodeo, arts, fry bread contest. October—Northern Navajo Fair, Shiprock, New Mexico; Western Navajo Fair, Tuba City. December—Navajo Nation Library Arts and Crafts Fair, Window Rock.

Navajo Nation Fair
Navajo Tourism Development Offices
P.O. Box 308N
Window Rock, AZ 86515
(602) 871-4941, ext. 1359 or 1360
Second weekend in September. Arts and crafts exhibits, intertribal powwow, traditional dances and singing.

Tumacacori Fiesta
Tumacacori National Monument
P.O. Box 67
Tumacacori, AZ 85640
(602) 398-2341
Native American and Mexican-American music, dancing, and singing. Demonstrations of traditional crafts; authentic food. Held at Mission San José de Tumacacori, December.

COLORADO

Annual Juried Indian and Western Art Show
Benefit for Southern Ute Cultural Center
Durango, CO 81301
(303) 563-4581
Arts and crafts, Indian dances, Native foods, craft demonstrations. Held in June in Buckley Park.

Colorado Indian Market
P.O. Box 13006
Boulder, CO 80308
(303) 447-9967
Festival of Native American Arts, culture, and cuisine. Exhibit of works by hundreds of Native Americans representing 90 nations. Craft demonstrations and sales. July.

Colorado Winter Indian Market
P.O. Box 13006
Boulder, CO 80308
(303) 447-9967
Gathering of more than 400 Native American artists representing 90 nations. Features art exhibits and demonstrations; sales of jewelry, Navajo rugs, Hopi kachina dolls, beadwork, quillwork, paintings, and sculpture; performances of traditional music and dance. Held at Currigan Exhibition Hall, November.

CONNECTICUT

Quinnehtukqut Rendezvous and Powwow
247 Tolland Street
East Hartford, CT 06108
(203) 282-1404
Rendezvous of more than 40 Native American groups for ceremonial dances; drumming competition. Reenactment of mountain man encampment, arts and crafts demonstrations, cooking of old-time foods. Held in August at Haddam Meadows State Park. Admission charge.

IDAHO

Annual Shoshone-Bannock Indian Festival and Rodeo
Shoshone-Bannock Tribal Council
Fort Hall Indian Reservation
P.O. Box 306
Fort Hall, ID 83202
(208) 238-3700
Parade, all-Indian rodeo, bareback riding, relay races, old-timers' rodeo, war dance competition, and exhibition dancing. August. Admission charge to some events.

INDIANA

Feast of the Hunters' Moon
Tippecanoe County Historical Association
909 South Street
Lafayette, IN 47901
(317) 742-8411
Reenactment of a mid-18th century fur-trading rendezvous on the banks of the Wabash River. French and Indian dances, period music, military drills, and food. Held at Fort Ouiatenon Historical Park. Admission charge. Held September/October.

KANSAS

Wah-Shun-Gah Days
Chamber of Commerce
117 West Main Street
P.O. Box 227
Council Grove, KS 66846
(316) 767-5413
Community celebration honoring the Kaw Indian Chief Wah-Shun-Gah. Powow with more than 300 Native Americans, medicine show, parade, street dance, raft float down the Neosho River, and trail cookout. June.

MINNESOTA

Annual Mankato Traditional Powwow
P.O. Box 61
Mankato State University
Mankato, MN 56001
(507) 388-4417 or 389-6125
Gathering of Native Americans at ancient Sioux ceremonial grounds, with social and ceremonial dancing, arts and crafts, food. Held at Land of Memories Park, September. Admission charge.

MISSISSIPPI

Choctaw Indian Fair
Chamber of Commerce
P.O. Box 51
Philadelphia, PA 39350
(601) 656-1742
Cultural programs; traditional arts, crafts, and dancing; stickball, archery, and food. Held at the Choctaw Indian Reservation, July. Admission charge.

MONTANA

Crow Fair
Little Big Horn College
Crow Agency, MT 59022
(406) 638-2228
Northern Plains Indian festival, with parades, games, crafts, dances, displays, and a rodeo. August. Admission charge to some events.

Northern American Indian Day
Blackfeet Tribal Council
Browning, MT 59417
(406) 338-7511, ext. 365
Four-day program of Indian dancing, games, sports events, an encampment, and parades. One of the largest gatherings of U.S. and Canadian Native Americans in the Northwest. At Blackfeet Tribal Fairgrounds. July.

Rocky Boy's Powwow
Rocky Boy's Reservation
Tribal Office
P.O. Box 544
Rocky Boy Route
Box Elder, MT 59521
(406) 395-4282

Groups from throughout the United States and Canada participate in dance competitions, games, ceremonials, and giveaways. August.

NEW MEXICO

Indian Pueblos
1. Eight Northern Indian Pueblos Council
   P.O. Box 969
   San Juan Pueblo, NM 87566
   (505) 852-4261
2. Five Sandoval Indian Pueblos, Inc.
   P.O. Box 580
   Bernalillo, NM

The Indian calendar year is marked by dances, feast days, and festivals, some of which are open to the public. For special events in New Mexico, contact the above Pueblo organizations.

Annual Benefit Auction of Indian Arts
Wheelwright Museum
704 Camino Lejo
Box 5153
Santa Fe, NM 87502
(505) 982-4636
Fourth weekend in August during Indian Market weekend.

Annual Eight Northern Indian Pueblo Artist and Craftsmen Show
Route 5, Box 315A
Santa Fe, NM 87501
On State Route 4 (Los Alamos Highway), 24 miles north of Santa Fe
(505) 852-4265
Scheduled third Saturday and Sunday in July. Over 600 North American Indian artists and craftsmen will sell their work. All items handmade; more than 300 booths. Traditional Pueblo and Plains dances.

Annual Indian Pueblo Cultural Center Craft Fair
Indian Pueblo Cultural Center
2401 12th NW
Albuquerque, NM 87102
(505) 843-7270
Forty to fifty booths display crafts of Pueblo Indians, traditional dances from various pueblos. Special events in July and from May to September.

Annual Indian Rodeo Finals
P.O. Box 8546
Albuquerque, NM 87198
(505) 265-1791
Held annually at New Mexico State Fairgrounds in November.

Crownpoint Navajo Rug Auction
Crownpoint Rug Weavers Association
P.O. Box 1630
Crownpoint, NM 87313
(505) 786-5302
A unique experience where weaver and buyer meet. Wide selection of Indian rugs from New Mexico and Arizona. Information on dates and location available through Crownpoint Elementary School.

Farmington Outdoor Historical Pageant
Lions Wilderness Park
4601 College Boulevard
Farmington, NM 87401
(505) 326-7602
"Anasazi, the Ancient Ones," two-hour pageant, 40 performances.

Gathering of the Nations Powwow
University Arena
University of Albuquerque
Albuquerque, NM 87106
(505) 831-1820
Mid-April dance competitions, arts and crafts, 5-and-10 K walk, Miss Indian World Contest.

High Country Arts and Crafts Fair
Picuris Tribal Office
P.O. Box 228
Peñasco, NM 87553
(505) 587-2519
Some 250 Indian, Hispanic, and Anglo artists and craftspeople take booths to sell handmade items, such as leather goods, quilts, jewelry, paintings, furniture, weaving, and pottery. July.

Indian Market
P.O. Box 1964
Santa Fe, NM 87501-1964
(505) 983-5220
Annual event held third weekend in August on the Santa Fe Plaza. Indian sculptors, weavers, jewelers, painters, and basket makers from all over the country set up booths for juried show.

65th Inter-Tribal Indian Ceremonial
Inter-Tribal Indian Ceremonial Association
P.O. Box 1
Church Rock, NM 87311
(505) 863-3896 or (800) 233-4528
Native Americans from across the country gather for ceremonial dances, traditional games, a parade, rodeo, outdoor and indoor marketplaces, and crafts demonstrations. Held at Red Rock State Park in August. Admission charge.

Taos Arts Festival
P.O. Box 2915
Taos, NM 87571
(505) 758-3872 or (800) 732-TAOS (outside state)
Tricultural arts extravaganza presenting Taos artists and craftsworkers. September–October.

NEW YORK

Annual Iroquois Indian Festival
Schoharie Museum of Iroquois Indians
Box 158
Schoharie, NY 12157
(518) 295-8553 or 234-2276
Festival features Iroquois arts and crafts. Demonstrations of social dancing, films and videos on Iroquois culture, Iroquois food. Labor Day weekend.

Annual Otsiningo Powwow
Roberson Center
40 Front Street
Binghamton, NY 13905
Festival of arts, crafts, dance, and history celebrating the Onondaga Nation. Craft and cooking demonstrations, historic photo exhibit on the Onondaga, dance performances. Over 50 craftspeople's work for sale.

Annual Turtle Powwow
Native American Center for the Living Arts
25 Rainbow Mall
Niagara Falls, NY 14303
(716) 284-2427
Prize money is offered as 250 dancers gather at the turtle-shaped art center. Third weekend in May.

Native American Harvest Celebration
The Turtle
25 Rainbow Mall
Niagara Falls, NY 14303
(716) 284-2427
November celebration of Native American crafts, foods, and ceremonies. Includes traditional Thanksgiving Day feast. Admission charge to some events.

NORTH DAKOTA

Annual United Tribes International Powwow
United Tribes Educational Technical Center
3315 South Airport Road
Bismarck, ND 58501
(701) 255-3285
Native Americans from 20 states and Canada compete in singing and dancing contests. Held in September. Admission charge.

OKLAHOMA

Annual American Indian Exposition
P.O. Box 908
Anadarko, OK 73005
(405) 247-5661
Five-day Indian fair. Indian dancing daily. Horse racing, parades, arts and crafts. Held in August.

Annual Guthrie USA Native American Celebration
Chamber of Commerce
P.O. Box 995
Guthrie, OK 73044
(405) 282-1947
Traditional song, dance, and drum contests; pageant, parade, concerts, art exhibits, crafts demonstrations, and rodeo. June. Admission charge.

Kiowa Blackleggings Warrior Society
c/o Southern Plains Indian Museum
Box 49
Anadarko, OK 73005
(405) 247-6221
Held at powwow grounds at Indian City in Anadarko.

Red Earth
Oklahoma City Convention and Tourism Bureau
4 Santa Fe Plaza
Oklahoma City, OK 73102
(405) 278-8900
(800) CALL-OKL
Native American celebration, annual three-day event held first week in June. Nations gather for dance competition, works of art featuring Native American artisans, Native American foods.

OREGON

Native American Days
Klamath County Museum
1451 Main Street
Klamath Falls, OR 97601
(503) 882-2501
Displays of historical artifacts, memorabilia, and native crafts; crafts sale and Native American food. August.

Pendleton Round-Up and Happy Canyon Pageant
Pendleton Round-Up Association
P.O. Box 609
Pendleton, OR 97801
(800) 824-1603 (Oregon); 800-524-2984 (outside)
Rodeo competitions, parade, Indian powwow, cowboy breakfast, and performances of Wild West pageant. A tipi village is assembled to be occupied by groups throughout the Pacific Northwest.

SOUTH DAKOTA

Annual Sisseton Wahpeton Sioux Tribal Fourth of July Powwow
Tribal Secretary
P.O. Box 509
Agency Village, SD 57262
(605) 398-3911
Native Americans from Western states and Canada compete in ceremonial dances. Native American crafts. July.

Oglala Nation Fair and Rodeo
Office of the Vice President
P.O. Box H
Pine Ridge, SD 57770
(605) 867-5821
Powwow, dancing contests, beauty pageant, rodeo, and children's games. Held at Oglala Sioux Veterans Memorial Park. July–August.

Red Cloud Indian Art Show
Heritage Center
Box 100
Pine Ridge, SD 57770
(605) 867-5888
Annual art show. Held all summer.

South Dakota Tribal Arts
Shirley A. Bordeaux
331 North Phillips
Sioux Falls, SD 57102
(605) 334-4060
Invitational art show and market sponsored by American Indian Services, a nonprofit organization. September.

TENNESSEE

Pinson Mounds State Archeological Area
4600 Ozier Road
Pinson, TN 38366
(901) 988-5614
Indian dances, movies on Indian legends. Arts and crafts from several groups, craft demonstrations. September.

WASHINGTON

Makah Indian Reservation
P.O. Box 115
Neah Bay, WA 98357
(206) 645-2201
Celebration of citizenship grant with traditional dances, salmon bake, games, and canoe races. August.

Yakima Indian National Cultural Center
P.O. Box 15, Dept. B
Toppenish, WA 98948
(509) 865-2800
Call for list of many events.

WEST VIRGINIA

Native American Week
Augusta Heritage Center
Davis and Elkins College
100 Sycamore Street
Elkins, WV 26241
(304) 636-1900
Annual workshop sessions to acquaint people with traditional music, dance, crafts, and folklore. Emphasis on Seneca, Shawnee, and Cherokee. Mid-July–mid-August.

WYOMING

Cheyenne Frontier Day
P.O. Box 2666
Cheyenne, WY 82003
(800) 227-6336
The West's oldest rodeo. Concurrent fine arts show and Western museum exhibit. July.

Fort Bridger Rendezvous
Evanston Chamber of Commerce
P.O. Box 365
Evanston, WY 82930
(307) 789-2757
September.

The Laubin Ancient Indian Dances
Grand Teton Lodge
Box 250
Moran, WY 83013
(307) 733-2811

CANADA

For powwows throughout Canada contact:

Native Development in Performing Arts and Visual Arts
27 Carlton Street, Suite 208
Toronto, ON M5B 1LE
(416) 977-2512
Also:

Ministry of Tourism, Recreation and Culture
675 Belleville Street
Victoria, BC V8V 1X4
(604) 387-2908

Indian Salmon Festival
P.O. Box 669
1715 Park Avenue
Prince Rupert, B.C. V8J 351
(604) 622-1717; 624-5637
Display of arts and crafts, native foods, traditional dances and songs. Held annually in June.

ARTISTS, ARTIFACTS, AND DEALERS

ALASKA

The Mt. Juneau Trading Post
151 South Franklin Street
Juneau, AK 99801
(907) 586-8426
Specializing in Native Alaskan crafts.

ARIZONA

Arrowsmith's
P.O. Box 2078
Prescott, AZ 86302
(602) 445-7196
American Indian art. Call for catalogue.

Cameron Trading Post
P.O. Box 83
Cameron, AZ 86020
(602) 679-2231
Historic Indian materials, many items of historic interest.

Desert House Crafts
2841 North Campbell Avenue
Tuscon, AZ 85719
(602) 323-2132
Southwest Indian Kachina dolls, rugs, jewelry, baskets, pottery, and carvings. African and Mexican arts and crafts.

Durfee Gallery
3618 Civic Center Plaza Road
Scottsdale, AZ 85251
(602) 946-4226
A selection of Indian and contemporary art in the Southwest.

Garland's Navajo Rugs
Highway 179
P.O. Box 851
Sedona, AZ 86336
(602) 282-4070
Buys direct from weavers. Kachina dolls by Hopis, baskets, sand paintings.

Hall's Indian Shop
Oak Creek Route, Box 200
Flagstaff, AZ 86001
(602) 282-3925
Navajo rugs, kachinas, pottery, baskets.

John C. Hill
P.O. Box 33666
6819 North 21st Avenue, Suite S
Phoenix, AZ 85067
(602) 249-1898
American folk art, American Indian art.

Louran Numkena
P.O. Box 2804
Tuba City, AZ 86045
(602) 283-6895
Hopi artist of kachina dolls.

Manfred Susunkewa
6914 West McKinley Street
Phoenix, AZ 85043
(602) 936-5244
Kachina maker.

Many Goats
4500 North Oracle Road
Tucson, AZ 85705-1603
(602) 887-0814
Authentic American Indian handcrafts.

Michael J. Bradford
P.O. Box 174
Cottonwood, AZ 86326
(602) 646-5596
Southwestern Indian art.

Morning Star Traders, Inc.
2020 East Speedway
Tucson, AZ 85719
(602) 881-2112 or 881-5161
Specializing in fine Southwestern Indian Art.

Pima Fashions
Route 2, Box 723
Gila River Indian Reservation
Laveen, AZ 85339
(602) 237-2938
Southwest Indian, designed clothing, fashion shows.

Rivas Bahti Gallery
4300 North Campbell, #20
Tucson, AZ 85718
(602) 577-0290
Indian arts.

She-He-Mu Crafts
Leon R. Myron
P.O. Box 2038
Keams Canyon, AZ 86034
(602) 738-5516
Hopi kachina doll carver.

Terry DeWald
8401-D East Ocotillo Drive
Tucson, AZ 85715
(602) 749-9790
Papago Indian baskets, Apache burden baskets, historic Southwest and California basketry, historic Navajo textiles.

CALIFORNIA

Alexanian Rugs
7848 Silverton, Suite G
San Diego, CA 92126
(619) 566-3833
Washing, restoration, color run removal, preservation of rugs, blankets, Saltillos.

Caskey Lees Gallery
Box 244
Venice, CA 90291
(213) 396-0876
Country furniture, Native arts and artifacts. Runs shows in San Francisco, Pasadena, and Los Angeles. Contact for specific information.

Coffman's Fine Arts
457 North Palm Canyon Drive, #5
P.O. Box 430
Palm Springs, CA 92263
(619) 325-0676
Museum-quality Indian artifacts, Western art, relics and collectibles. Buy, sell, and appraise.

Don Bennett & Assoc.
P.O. Box 283
Agoura, CA 91301
(818) 991-5596
Dealers and appraisers of American Indian art. Produces American Indian Art Auction Seminars. Sponsors Annual Santa Fe, New Mexico, Invitational Antique American Indian Art Show and Sale in August.

Gary Spratt
P.O. Box 162
Rutherford, CA 94573
(707) 963-4022
North American Indian art, American country furniture, American primitive art.

Hyde and Seek Antiques
1913 Hyde Street, near Union Street
San Francisco, CA 94109
(415) 776-8865
Vintage clothing and accessories, decorative and folk art, American Indian artifacts.

Jerome Evans Gallery
1826 Capital Avenue
Sacramento, CA 95814
(916) 448-3759
Traditional and contemporary art of the Native Peoples of North and South America, Africa, and the Pacific Islands. Write for schedule of special sales. Also has gallery in Lake Tahoe.

Kim Martindale
P.O. Box 141
Agoura, CA 91301
(818) 889-5187
American Indian art, Oriental art.

Louis Newman Galleries
322 North Beverly Drive
Beverly Hills, CA 90210
(213) 278-6311
Exhibits work of Doug Hyde, sculptor.

Maid in America
736 Alta Vista
Mill Valley, CA 94941
(415) 388-2245
Folk art, antiques, and American Indian art.

Many Horses Gallery
740 North La Cienega Boulevard
Los Angeles, CA 90069
(213) 659-0737 or 659-0802
Fine arts of the Southwest.

Mountain Lion Trading Post
229 Avenue I, #150
Redondo Beach, CA 90277
(213) 540-4428
Southwestern arts, antiques, Indian and folk art, jewelry, furniture.

Nonesuch Gallery
1211 Montana Avenue
Santa Monica, CA 90403
(213) 393-1245
Art and antiques, Southwest, Americana primitives, American Indian artifacts, cowboy relics.

Tony Berlant
1304 12th Street
Santa Monica, CA 90401
(213) 395-5678
Navajo rugs.

Tribal Beginnings
6761 Sebastopol Avenue
c/o Gravenstein Station
Sebastopol, CA 95472
(707) 829-2174
Specializing in classic Navajo textiles and offering other antique and contemporary Native American art.

Two Bears Gallery
13263 Ventura Boulevard, #8
Studio City, CA 91604
(818) 906-8235
Contemporary Southwestern art and jewelry.

Walt Moreau
P.O. Box 14764
San Francisco, CA 94114
(415) 861-8319
American Indian art. Collections purchased, appraisals.

COLORADO

Mark Winter
P.O. Box 1570
Pagosa Springs, CO 81147
(303) 264-5957
Indian blankets.

Native American Trading Company
1301 Bannock
Denver, CO 80204
(303) 534-0771
A gallery of fine Southwest and Native American art.

The Squash Blossom
2531 West Colorado Avenue
Colorado Springs, CO 80904
(303) 632-1899
Pottery, kachinas.

DISTRICT OF COLUMBIA

Indian Craft Shop
1800 C Street NW
Room 1023, U.S. Dept. of Interior
Washington, DC 20240
(202) 343-4056 or 737-4381
Baskets, Navajo rugs, dolls, kachinas, Alaskan Native crafts, carvings.

FLORIDA

Four Winds Gallery
1167 Third Street South
The Corner Building
Olde Naples, FL 33940
(813) 263-7555
Indian art.

Royal Palm Hammock
P.O. Box 122
Marco Island, FL 33937-0122
(813) 394-5246
The Indian chikee builders, any size and any type. Also repair and reroofing.

MARYLAND

Nostalgia Stations
1000 Light Street
Baltimore, MD 21230
(301) 837-3625
Manufactures Mimbreno tableware, based on Mary Cotler's original Santa Fe Railroad designs.

MASSACHUSETTS

Colleen C. James
Route 20
Sturbridge, MA 01566
(617) 347-2744 or 798-8569
Native American art and selected Americana.

Skinner, Inc.
Route 117
Boltin, MA 01740
(508) 779-5528
Auctioneers and appraisers of American Indian and ethnographic art.

MINNESOTA

The Raven Gallery
3827 West 50th Street
Minneapolis, MN 55410
(612) 925-4474
Inuit sculpture, Indian and Eskimo art. Color photos available.

MONTANA

Blue Star
300 West Main
Missoula, MT 59802
(406) 728-1738
Makers of canvas tipis.

Custer Battlefield Trading Post
P.O. Box 246
Crow Agency, MT 59022
(406) 638-2270
Gifts, relics, Indian arts and crafts.

Col. Doug Allard
P.O. Box 46
St. Ignatius, MT 59865
(406) 745-2951
Indian art from the area.

Dwight B. Billedeaux
Box 532
Ronan, MT 59864
(406) 644-2267
Native sculptor in metal.

Native American Art & Artifacts
2622 Broadwater Avenue
Billings, MT 59102
(406) 656-5707
Baskets, pottery, beadwork, stoneware; prehistoric, historic, contemporary. By appointment only.

Signs-4-U
by Johnny Arlee
P.O. Box 163
Arlee, MT 59821
Flathead Indian scenes; hand-lettering, airbrushing, murals, banners, windows.

NEW MEXICO

Alan Kessler
305 Camino Cerrito
Santa Fe, NM 87501
(505) 986-1017
Fine American Indian art of the Plains, Southwest, and Woodlands peoples.

Allison Bird
P.O. Box 884
San Juan Pueblo, NM 87566
(505) 753-7692
Professional research services, American Indian/Spanish Colonial.

Andrew Nagen
P.O. Box 1306
Corrales, NM 87048
(505) 898-5058
Old Navajo rugs.

Bead World
4931 Prospect NE
Albuquerque, NM 87110
(505) 884-3133
Manufacturers of quality silver beads, findngs and castings, seed beads, semiprecious stone and fossil round beads, ovals, turquoise, *heishi.* Looms and beading supplies. Sales and mail-order. Wholesale, retail, jobber.

Bill and Mary Martin
P.O. Box 35
Cochiti, NM 87041
(505) 465-2426
Pueblo drums and storytellers.

The Blue Corn Connection
8812 Fourth Street
Albuquerque, NM 87114
(505) 897-2412
Sells a variety of blue corn products, including pancake and waffle mixes and blue popcorn.

Buffalo Dancer Gallery
Plaza Real (east side of Plaza)
Taos, NM 87571
(505) 758-8718
Santa Clara black pottery, old Navajo rugs, beadwork, kachinas, Hopi and Navajo jewelry.

Canfield
414 Canyon Road
Santa Fe, NM 87504
(505) 988-4199
Specializes in antique Indian art. By appointment.

Casados Farms
Box 852
San Juan Pueblo, NM 87566
(505) 852-2433
Sells blue corn and blue cornmeal.

Channing-Dale-Throckmorton
Upstairs on the Plaza
53 Old Santa Fe Trail
Santa Fe, NM 87501
(505) 984-2133
Fine arts of Native peoples.

Christopher Selser
P.O. Box 9328
Santa Fe, NM 87504
(505) 984-1481
Showing American Indian antiquities at:
Zaplin-Lampert Gallery
651 Canyon Road
Santa Fe, NM 87501
(505) 982-6100

Clarence Lee and Erecka Lee
142 Lincoln Avenue, Suite 836
Santa Fe, NM 87501
(505) 982-0385
Navajo jewelry.

C. McHorse
P.O. Box 8638
Santa Fe, NM 87504
(505) 989-7716
Hand-built pottery and micaceous Taos clay pottery.

Cresencia Tafoya
Santa Clara Pueblo
Box 612
Espanola, NM 87532
(505) 753-4868
Pottery from Santa Clara Pueblo.

Cristof's
106 West San Francisco Street
Santa Fe, NM 87501
(505) 988-9881
Navajo rug gallery; sculpture, paintings, kachinas.

Dan Namingha
1113 Buckman Road
Santa Fe, NM 87501
(505) 988-5091
Hopi painter.

D'Aumell
924 Paseo de Peralta, Suite 1
Santa Fe, NM 87501
(505) 988-7050
Native American art and artifacts.

David P. Bradley
P.O. Box 5692
Santa Fe, NM 87502
Native American painter.

Davis Mather Folk Art Gallery
141 Lincoln Avenue
Santa Fe, NM 87501
(505) 983-1660 or 988-1218
Navajo pictorial rugs, including flag rugs; New Mexican folk art; pictorials by Fannie Mann.

Denise Wallace
Studio of Denise and Samuel Wallace
825 Early Street, Suite D
Santa Fe, NM 87501
(505) 984-0265
Jewelry makers. Also represented at El Parian de Santa Fe Gallery.

Dewey Galleries Limited
74 East San Francisco Street
Santa Fe, NM 87501
(505) 982-8632
Fine American Western art, pottery, jewelry, representational painting and sculpture. Exhibits work of Cippy Crazy Horse, silver jeweler, and jewelers Gail Bird and Yazzie Johnson.

El Parian de Santa Fe
116 West San Francisco Street
Plaza Mercado, Suite 204
Santa Fe, NM 87501
(505) 984-3150
Contemporary Southwest Indian material. Exhibits the work of Denise Wallace, jewelry maker, and Rhonda Holy Bear, doll maker (Sioux nation). Also features work of Santa Fe potter Jackie Stevens.

Forrest Fenn Gallery
1075 Paseo de Peralta
Santa Fe, NM 87501
(505) 982-4631
Specializes in paintings by old Taos and Santa Fe artists and masters of the American west. Bronze and stone sculpture, old pottery, baskets, beadwork, jewelry, and other artifacts of the American Indian.

Foutz Trading Co.
P.O. Box 1894
Shiprock, NM 87420
(505) 368-5790
Wholesale and retail, specializing in Navajo rugs and sandpaintings.

Gabe Yellowbird and Katy Trujillo
P.O. Box 72
Cochiti, NM 87041
(505) 862-7252
Cochiti drums and black pottery. Storytellers.

Galeria Capistrano
409 Canyon Road
Santa Fe, NM 87501
(505) 984-3024
Southwestern art and Native American painting, sculpture, jewelry, and pottery. Exhibits the work of Frank La Pena, painter.

Gary Yazzie Fine Arts
P.O. Box 73
Prewitt, NM 87045
(505) 287-3535
Navajo painter.

Glenn Green Gallery
50 East San Francisco Street
Santa Fe, NM 87501
(505) 988-4168
Exclusive representatives for Allan Houser, sculptor in bronze and stone.

Has other galleries in Scottsdale and Phoenix.

Hansen Gallery
923 Paseo de Peralta
Santa Fe, NM 87501
(505) 983-2336
Antiques and fine Indian art.

Harold Littlebird
P.O. Box 4612
Santa Fe, NM 87502
(505) 983-1546
Ceramic artist.

Indian Arts and Crafts Association
4215 Lead SE
Albuquerque, NM 87108
(505) 265-9149
Sponsors wholesale market for retailers. Native American Indian crafts and pottery.

James Reid, Ltd.
112 East Palace Avenue
Santa Fe, NM 87501
(505) 988-1147
Antique and contemporary arts, featuring designs from gallery workshop; specializing in belts, belt buckles, and earrings. Gallery features eight silversmiths and three leathersmiths, each providing individual designs.

J. B. Tanner Trading Company
3600-D Menaul NE
Albuquerque, NM 87110
(505) 884-1056
Navajo rugs, jewelry, sandpaintings, kachinas, and pottery.

Joe and Eliza Chavez
Box 254
Santo Domingo Pueblo, NM 87052
(505) 465-2392
Handmade beads: turquoise, *heishi,* melon shell, turtle shell, coral.

Joe V. and Elizabeth Trujillo
P.O. Box 1017
San Juan Pueblo, NM 87566
Hand-carved traditional dance figures.

John J. Kania
924 Paseo de Peralta
Santa Fe, NM 87501
(505) 982-8767 (gallery), 982-5251 (home)
Traditional Native American arts. Member Appraisers Association of America.

Karen Kinnett Hyatt
P.O. Box 1113
Santa Fe, NM 87504
(505) 984-8000
Handwoven textiles by Ramona Sakiestewa.

Lane Coulter
123 East San Mateo
Sante Fe, NM 87501
(505) 984-8672 or 988-2905
Southwestern antiques and American Indian art. By appointment.

Lanford-Gilmore
924 Paseo de Peralta
Santa Fe, NM 87501
(505) 989-9115

Marilyn Butler Fine Art Gallery
225 Galisteo
Santa Fe, NM 87501
(505) 988-5387
Exhibits work of Native American painters Emmi Whitehorse and Jaune Quick-to-See Smith.

Mark E. Hooper
3825 Anderson SE
Albuquerque, NM 87108
(505) 256-0321
American Indian jewelry, beadwork, ethnographics.

Mary Lewis
Box 467
Pueblo of Acoma, NM 87034
(505) 552-9692
Acoma pottery. Daughter of Lucy Lewis.

Mayo-Tope Gallery, Ltd.
415 Canyon Road
Santa Fe, NM 87501
(505) 982-9500
American Indian art, artifacts, pictographic art.

Morning Star Gallery
513 Canyon Road
Santa Fe, NM 87501
(505) 982-8187
Deals exclusively in antique Indian art, 19th-century Plains Indians art, Western paintings.

Mudd-Carr Gallery
227 Otero
Santa Fe, NM 87501
(505) 982-8206
Pre-1900 Navajo weavings, Pueblo pottery, Spanish Colonial art, fine Indian art. Appraisal service.

Native Plant Materials
P.O. Box 57
Cerrillos, NM 87010
(505) 473-0407
Sells dried plant materials native to the area.

Packard's Indian Trading Co., Inc.
61 Old Santa Fe Trail
Santa Fe, NM 87501
(505) 983-9241
Indian pottery, jewelry, rugs, drums, and moccasins.

Prairie Edge
102 East Water Street
Santa Fe, NM 87501
(505) 984-1336
Examples of mounted buffalo skulls, bow and arrow sets, knives, painted buffalo and elk robes, bone jewelry, silver jewelry. Handmade with authentic materials.

Preservation
Gerald Lamb, proprietor
P.O. Box 9702
Santa Fe, NM 87504
(505) 984-2277
Restores and preserves fine ethnographic and folk art antiquities.

Rain Parrish
535 Cordova Road, Suite 250
Santa Fe, NM 87501
(505) 984-8236
Native American art consultant.

R. C. Gorman's Navajo Gallery
Off Ledoux, southwest of the Plaza
Taos, NM 87571
(505) 758-3250
Featuring works of Navajo painter R. C. Gorman.

Rettig & Martinez Gallery
418 Montezuma
P.O. Box 8526
Santa Fe, NM 87504
(505) 983-4640
Exhibits work of Robert Haozous, sculptor.

Richard M. Howard
1012 Foothills Trail
Santa Fe, NM 87505
(505) 983-9566
American Indian art; contemporary and historic pottery.

Richardson Trading Co. and Cash Pawn, Inc.
222-28 West 66 Avenue
Gallup, NM 87301
(505) 722-4762
Indian arts and crafts.

Robert F. Nichols
419 Canyon Road
Santa Fe, NM 87501
(505) 982-2145
American Indian art, American folk art.

Santa Fe East
200 Old Santa Fe Trail
Santa Fe, NM 87501
(505) 988-3103
Silver, rugs, sculpture, one-of-a-kind jewelry, Native American pueblo pottery.

Santa Fe Pendleton
On the Plaza
53 Old Santa Fe Trail
Santa Fe, NM 87501
(505) 983-5855
Pendleton blankets and products.

The Silverman Collection
P.O. Box 2610
Santa Fe, NM 87504-2610
(505) 982-6722
Collection of Navajo and Pueblo blankets and textiles, Acoma dolls, and other historic and prehistoric Native American artifacts.

Southwestern Restorations
P.O. Box 14263
Albuquerque, NM 87191
(505) 292-5612
Reweaving, buying, and selling of antique and contemporary textiles, Navajo rugs, blankets, and Classic weavings.

Streets of Taos
200 Canyon Road
Santa Fe, NM 87501
(505) 983-8268
Old and new Navajo jewelry and pottery, Santa Fe shirts and paintings.

Taos Indian Drums
Box 1916
Taos, NM 87571
(505) 758-3796
Fine selection from America's oldest drum-making tradition.

Tobe Turpen's Indian Trading Co.
1710 South Second Street
Gallup, NM 87301
(505) 722-3806
Fine Indian arts and crafts: jewelry, rugs, pottery, baskets, kachinas, moccasins, sandpaintings. Collectors' items.

Tony Reyna's Shops 1 and 2
Taos, NM 87571
Kachina Lodge 2
(505) 758-2142
Taos Pueblo Lodge 1
(505) 758-3855
Southwest Indian arts and crafts at Indian-owned and -operated shops.

Two Grey Hills Gallery
6927 Guadalupe Trail
Albuquerque, NM 87107
(505) 344-3668
Southwest Native American art. By appointment.

Yazzie Johnson/Gail Bird
Box 511
Ojo Caliente, NM 87549
(505) 583-2282
Unique contemporary Indian jewelry in brass, gold, and silver.

NEW YORK

Algonquin Arts and Crafts
1736 Mt. Hope Road
Lewiston, NY 14092
(716) 297-3823
Beadwork by Ann Green.

Calvin Kettle
Box 101
Lawtons, NY 14091
Makes lacrosse sticks and turtle rattles.

Eleanor Tulman Hancock, Inc.
202 Riverside Drive
New York, NY 10025
(212) 866-5267
North American Indian art.

Peter Jones
Cattaraugus Indian Reservation
Box 174
Versailles, NY 14168
(716) 532-5993
Pottery.

Sotheby's
Dr. Bernard de Grunne
Director of Tribal Art Department
1334 York Avenue
New York, NY 10021
(212) 606-7325
Information about buying and selling.

Tessie Snow
R.D.1, Box J13
Salamanca, NY 14779
(716) 945-4944 or 945-1790 (Seneca Nation)
Cornhusk doll maker.

OHIO

Terry Schafer
Route 2, Box 270
Marietta, OH 45750
(614) 374-2807
Fine American Indian art: baskets, beaded items, blankets, pottery.

OKLAHOMA

Anna B. Mitchell
P.O. Box 195
Vinita, OK 74301
(918) 256-3702
Traditional Cherokee potter.

Marcus Anerman
3913 NW 15th Street
Oklahoma City, OK 73107
(405) 948-1768
Beadwork.

Mavis Doering
5918 NW 58th Street
Oklahoma City, OK 73122
(405) 787-6082
Cherokee baskets.

Paukeigope (Strikes the Enemy Down in Running Water)
Box 1101
Anadarko, OK 73005
(405) 643-5075
Cradleboards, tipis, dresses, leggings, shirts, lances, bow cases, shields.

OREGON

Arthur W. Erickson, Inc.
1030 SW Taylor
Portland, OR 97205
(503) 227-4710
Indian and Eskimo arts and textiles, paintings, and ivory.

Natalie Fay Linn
2222 NW Lovejoy, Room 504A
Portland, OR 97210
(503) 292-1177
Indian baskets.

SOUTH DAKOTA

Pioneer Trading Co.
246 South Chicago
Hot Springs, SD 57747
(605) 745-5252
Pawnshop: buy, sell, trade antiques, secondhand and old Indian and Western items.

TEXAS

American Indian Art
P.O. Box 26173
Austin, TX 78755
(512) 453-0367
Lectures, acquisitions, consignments.

Bruce M. Shackelford
P.O. Box 15707
San Antonio, TX 78212
(512) 732-7311
American Indian art, appraisals, Western Americana, American collections. By appointment.

Jack Dulaney Trading Co.
130 North Stevens, #D
El Paso, TX 79905
(915) 544-7574 or 581-7922
Primitive Indian art, Mexican imports, Colonial furniture. Appraising service.

Waterbird Traders
3420 Greenville Avenue
Dallas, TX 75206
(214) 821-4606
Fine American Indian, Spanish Colonial, primitive art, and antiques.

WASHINGTON

Bruce Boyd
P.O. Box 20252
Seattle, WA 98102
(206) 322-8516
Buy, sell, appraise fine American Indian, Eskimo, Oceanic, and African art.

Don Delooska
5618 Lewis River Road
Ariel, WA 98603
(206) 225-9522
Mask maker.

George David
P.O. Box 141
Neah Bay, WA 98357
Sculptor, jeweler, mask maker.

Greg Colfax
P.O. Box 327
Neah Bay, WA 98357
Sculptor and mask maker.

Medicine Valley Trading Co.
P.O. Box 289
Toppenish, WA 98948
(509) 865-5838
Antiques, American Indian artifacts, and primitive art.

Spencer McCarty
P.O. Box 762
Neah Bay, WA 98357
(206) 645-2564
Sculptor and mask maker.

CANADA

Arts of the Raven Gallery
1015 Douglas Street
Victoria, BC V8W 2C5
(604) 386-3069
Contemporary Northwest Coast Indian art. Features masks, Eskimo soapstone carvings, prints.

Art Thompson
2721 Fifth Street
Victoria, BC V8T 4B1
(604) 384-9118
Specializes in West Coast–style poles, masks, rattles, prints, gold and silver jewelry.

Dorothy Grant
505 194th Street
Surrey, BC V3S 5J9
Textile artist, Northwest Coast.

Eagle of the Dawn Artist, Ltd.
Robert Davidson
16541 Upper Beach Road, R.R. 7
White Rock, BC V4B 5A8
(604) 536-2949
Graphic artist, mask maker, and totem pole carver.

Inuit Gallery
345 Water Street
Vancouver, BC V6B 1B8
(604) 688-7323
Indian and Inuit art, including Northwest Coast masks, wood carvings, carved and painted boxes, prints, and blankets; Eskimo soapstone sculptures, prints, drawings, tapestries, and artifacts.

Leona Lattimer
1590 West Second Avenue
Vancouver, BC V6J 1H2
(604) 732-4556
Specializes in Northwest Coast Indian art, appraisals; repairs argillite. Exhibits the work of Art Thompson, Vancouver Island sculptor, and Bill Reid, sculptor from Vancouver.

Walter Banko Enterprises, Ltd.
Box 97, Westmount P.O.
Montreal, QU H3Z 2T1
(514) 445-0712
Antique Indian art.

INDEX